P9-BVM-347

identity crisis in higher education

"The most pervasive aspect of the contemporary crisis on campus is a crisis of identity. People no longer seem to know who they are or how they can fit productively into social structures. As we move into postindustrial society, it is becoming clearer that the new life styles and ways of seeing (understanding Eastern philosophy and thought, emphasizing affective as well as cognitive dimensions of experience, living in today rather than in tomorrow, using drugs to heighten experience) are doing battle with the established values of colleges and universities. Yet many campuses are changing, and the world of scholarship is being altered.

"*Identity Crisis in Higher Education* is a cogent analysis of the current campus crisis of identity, both for persons and for structures. It tries to tell how and why campuses can change and are changing by focusing on two questions: How can higher education modify its characteristic educational intentions and practices in order to help students develop capacities for making intelligent normative commitments as well as for establishing critical detachment? What civic identity should and could higher education assume in relation to its involvement in the critical social and cultural issues of our time and to other institutional agencies? From the beginning of our inquiry, we have assumed that the traditional intellectual style of

lytical fragmentation
ent from moral issues
he increasing needs of
nts for an education
quate moral commit-
we have assumed that
cation is at its deepest
differing values, and
er ways in which the
ough which we seem
made a productive
ve force in changing
tion.

Higher Education
yone who has looked
on of values and atti-
is searching for some
on in which higher
n culture are moving.
nt for administrators
people. It gives some
ne nature of the gen-
may be breached; it
re disaffected because
tly; and it tells how
r the better."

—*from the* Preface

TORS

is research educator
ch and Development
d lecturer in educa-
fornia, Berkeley. He
d Authority (Jossey-

executive director of
College Work, Cam-

Identity Crisis in Higher Education

Harold L. Hodgkinson

Myron B. Bloy, Jr.

Editors

IDENTITY CRISIS IN HIGHER EDUCATION

Jossey-Bass Inc., Publishers
615 Montgomery Street · San Francisco · 1971

IDENTITY CRISIS IN HIGHER EDUCATION
Harold L. Hodgkinson and Myron B. Bloy, Jr., Editors

Jossey-Bass, Inc., Publishers
615 Montgomery Street
San Francisco, California 94111

Library of Congress Catalog Card Number 78-110644

International Standard Book Number ISBN 0-87589-085-7

Manufactured in the United States of America
Composed and printed by York Composition Company, Inc.
Bound by Chas. H. Bohn & Co., Inc.

JACKET DESIGN BY WILLI BAUM, SAN FRANCISCO

FIRST EDITION

Code 7036

The Jossey-Bass Series in Higher Education

General Editors

JOSEPH AXELROD
San Francisco State College
and University of California, Berkeley

MERVIN B. FREEDMAN
San Francisco State College
and Wright Institute, Berkeley

Preface

The most pervasive aspect of the contemporary crisis on campus is a crisis of identity. People no longer seem to know who they are or how they can fit productively into social structures. As we move into postindustrial society, it is becoming clearer that the new life styles and ways of seeing (understanding Eastern philosophy and thought, emphasizing affective as well as cognitive dimensions of experience, living in today rather than in tomorrow, using drugs to heighten experience) are doing battle with the established values of colleges and universities. Yet many campuses are changing, and the world of scholarship is being altered.

Identity Crisis in Higher Education is a cogent analysis of the current campus crisis of identity, both for persons and for structures. It tries to tell how and why campuses can and are changing by focusing on two questions: How can higher education modify its characteristic educational intentions and practices in order to help students develop capacities for making intelligent normative commitments as well as for establishing critical detachment? What civic identity should and could higher education assume in relation to its involvement in the critical social and cultural issues of our time and to other institutional agencies? From the beginning of our inquiry, we have assumed that the traditional intellectual style of higher education—analytical fragmentation of reality and detachment from moral issues—is not responsive to the increasing needs of some of the best students for an education and for personally adequate moral commitments. In other words, we have assumed that the crisis of higher education is at its deepest level a conflict between differing values, and we have tried to discover ways in which the cultural revolution through which we seem to be passing can be made a productive rather than a destructive force in changing American higher education.

Identity Crisis in Higher Education should be useful to anyone who has looked carefully at the confusion of values and attitudes on campuses and is searching for some clues as to the direction in which higher education and American culture are moving. It is particularly relevant for administrators and student personnel people. It gives some very good clues as to the nature of the generation gap and how it may be breached; it explains that students are disaffected because they see things differently; and it tells how we can change things for the better.

The project which resulted in the publication of this book was funded by the Danforth Foundation and was carried out by the Church Society for College Work under its director, Myron B. Bloy, Jr. As part of this study of the normative dilemma of higher education, the ten people whose papers appear in *Identity Crisis in Higher Education* met recently as a seminar for four weekends under the chairmanship of Joseph L. Walsh, the associate director of the Church Society. Sherry Hennesy was secretary for the project. We are deeply grateful to them for their contribution to the seminar, to the seminar members both for their papers and for their intense involvement in the seminar, and to the Danforth Foundation for making the project possible.

Berkeley, California
Cambridge, Massachusetts
November, 1970

HAROLD L. HODGKINSON
MYRON B. BLOY, JR.

Contents

Authors

MYRON B. BLOY, JR., executive director, Church Society for College Work, and lecturer, Massachusetts Institute of Technology

DANIEL CALLAHAN, director, Institute of Society, Ethics, and the Life Sciences

HAROLD L. HODGKINSON, project director, Center for the Study of Higher Education, University of California at Berkeley

LAWRENCE C. HOWARD, dean, Graduate School of Public and International Affairs, University of Pittsburgh

JOHN DAVID MAGUIRE, president, State College of New York at Old Westbury

EDWARD SCHWARTZ, graduate student, Brandeis University

EDWARD JOSEPH SHOBEN, JR., executive vice-president, The Evergreen State University

PAUL SPIKE, undergraduate, Columbia University

RUEL W. TYSON, JR., professor of religion, University of North Carolina

RICHARD WERTZ, assistant professor of humanities, coordinator of Seminar on Social Inquiry, Massachusetts Institute of Technology

Identity Crisis in Higher Education

Harold L. Hodgkinson
Myron B. Bloy, Jr.

The Identity Crisis

PROLOGUE

The expression *identity crisis,* first brought into common usage by Erik Erikson, is usually applied to individuals who, at some state of their development, find the prevailing cultural norms and necessities out of joint with what they feel as human beings. When a man feels at one with his culture, he does not need to raise questions about it. The essential component of identity crisis is that the individual is no longer sure of his relation to cultural norms. The chapters in this book contend that the expression *identity crisis* applies not only to individuals but to institutions and societies as well. In fact, there is a reciprocal relationship across the categories of identity crisis; as the sociologist Robert Merton once observed, society gets the crime rate that it deserves.

These chapters represent a year-long attempt to come to grips with the problem of the identity crisis of higher education from three perspectives: that of the individual, that of the university, and that of the society itself. The authors were selected for a series of seminars, each lasting two and one-half days, conducted during the 1968–69 academic year. Financial support for the program, which was administered through the Church Society for College Work, came from the Danforth Foundation, to whom we express our gratitude.

The chapters represent no attempt at consensus. Rather, each member of the seminar was encouraged to develop his own style of attack on the problem of the identity crisis in higher education. It was, however, a real seminar in every sense of the word, and individuals clearly learned from each other. Like most seminars, this one had its greatest interaction and excitement during our discussions and debates, in which we keyed off on each other's comments at will. As one would expect with a group as diverse as this, one of our major challenges was simply to understand one another. This was, we think, accomplished to a high degree. It is unfortunate that the reader is left with only the mortal remains of our discussions—that is, with the chapter each person developed as a consequence of his participation in the seminar. Nevertheless, it is our hope and conviction that these chapters serve a useful function in the developing literature of higher education in America.

The chapters are arranged here in three major categories, although the seminar did not expressly follow these categories. The three rubrics we have chosen for analytical purposes are the changing intellectual commitments of the university (Part One), the processes of change (Part Two), and the new consciousness and higher education (Part Three). These are all vitally important and related topics in higher education today.

It seems clear that major changes are occurring in the structure and content of intellectuality in university life. Common charges against universities are that the university concerns itself entirely with fact and has no concern for the value or affective component of human life; that the university, in its efforts to be pluralistic and value-free, refuses to take a stand on matters of conscience and thus loses any possibility of being a reconstruction agent in society; that the values of research have so dominated the institution that it has largely lost its pedagogical function except at the highest reaches of graduate school; that the university has become so concerned with vocationalism that its role is primarily one of certifying people for entrance into the meritocracy rather than one of trying to expand and enlarge the individual's awareness of the relationship between his processes of reflection and his experience. Our three authors in Part One come at the problem from very different perspectives and yet emerge with some important common judgments.

The chapter by Daniel Callahan is probably the most specifically grounded of the three in this part. He concerns himself almost entirely with the supposed distinction between facts and values, pointing out that this distinction is at the heart of many of our contemporary difficulties regarding the role and function of the university. He thoroughly refutes the fact-value distinction and points out that the notion of neutrality of the university is due primarily to its preoccupation with so-called facts, but very little attention is given to the criteria whereby certain facts—represented by certain social classes—are selected for inclusion in university life and other facts are neglected. Callahan's chapter mentions an interesting contradiction: The distinction between fact and value has been rather thoroughly discredited by philosophers for a long time, and yet the university continues to maintain the existence of this dichotomy. Callahan recommends that university structures be revised in such a way that universities reward those whose primary interest is in the area of values, rather than reject them or force them to resort to a somewhat phony empiricism. Value-centered curricula could be developed. Criteria for rewarding faculty members might be based as much on their ability to analyze values as on their ability to manipulate facts. Students could also be rewarded for their promotion of the dialectical relationship between so-called facts and so-called values.

One of the problems immediately relevant to Callahan's chapter forms the central thesis of Ruel W. Tyson's chapter. A great many of us who have done some reading in the history of education know that it appears that we have been this way before, that the road we are now traveling is not an entirely new one. There were, after all, large-scale student demonstrations a century ago, and the largest demonstrations ever seen on the Berkeley campus occurred shortly before World War I. Tyson points out very specifically that the two traditions at work in the current scene are the romantic tradition and the tradition of the Enlightenment. He suggests, in a perceptive analysis, that the current conflict may end up being just another war between "the clerks and the men of feeling." He points out that both traditions are dependent on each other and that the counter-culture which forms the basis for discussion in some other chapters in this book is really nothing more than an updated version of a very old quarrel. He uses Freud as a model for the convergence and divergence of the cultural styles that form the framework of his chapter. Freud was, of course, a product of the Enlightenment, yet in his interest and experience, his spontaneity, and his yearning for the unattainable he is clearly in the romantic tradition, at least partially. Tyson's analysis is particularly perceptive in explaining how it is that students seem to enjoy violent demonstrations: not as rationality, and not as politics, but as a kind of esthetic experience.

The third chapter in this part, by Edward Joseph Shoben, explores the central relationship between the university and the society in which it operates. Shoben, an accomplished observer and practitioner on the educational scene, believes firmly that ideas have consequences and that these consequences can be of many kinds. He is also keenly aware that universities often do a number of seemingly contradictory things simultaneously. From his analysis of the relationships between the institution of higher education and the society, Shoben draws an interesting conclusion which is often mentioned but seldom followed through—conflicts within the contemporary university mirror conflicts in the country as a whole. Thus if an individual on a campus is denied intellectual freedom to pursue truth as he sees it, it is only a matter of time before the same trait will emerge in a larger context.

Shoben is particularly persuasive on the concept of the university as a tenuous and uneasy balance between competing forces. This balance must be maintained because of the delicacy of an institution devoted to the free exploration of ideas. It is also clear to

Shoben that an institution devoted to this exploration of ideas cannot run its student activities as if students were simply robots or servants. He suggests that if the right of privacy, the right of free inquiry, and the right to gather in public forums to discuss ideas are rights which follow unequivocally from the university's intellectual commitments, a university should be organized around its intellectual commitments. This, in the first place, has never occurred recently, and, in the second place, could be the focus of a powerful effort to change current university structures. If the university is to be pluralistic and attract people of diverse backgrounds, then clearly its programs for intellectual and personal development must also be pluralistic. There are quite clearly some moral principles which follow from the university's commitment to the pursuit of knowledge and to the ability of individuals to reflect productively on their own experience in order to answer more clearly the questions of who they are and what is the nature of their society. Clearly we have a long way to go in putting into practice the moral perspectives which, Shoben rightly points out, are an absolute consequence of our commitment to certain values within the university setting.

The chapters in Part Two reflect four perspectives on the major change in higher education. Harold L. Hodgkinson's utopia, "Walden U.," is in one sense a continuation of Shoben's paper in that it provides the structure for a utopian institution based entirely upon certain commitments as to the nature of learning. It is an attempt to show what an institution would look like if all the nuts and bolts of its organizational patterns added up to a commitment to a certain kind of learning—learning based on inquiry. Although the conception is utopian, there is no reason, financial or political, why such an institution as Walden U. could not be created tomorrow if we wished to do so. Many utopias are structured to point out what the institution will not do in relation to other institutions of higher education in America. Walden is designed with a positive imperative in that it can do certain things which are not being accomplished by other institutions. We begin with a utopia because all efforts at change are moving toward something and it seemed interesting to begin with a conception of what might be—tomorrow if we wish.

However, in terms of getting from here to there we must be aware of some strategies which are productive of change and others which are not. In this area, John David Maguire has written a fascinating recipe for change, stating some general principles that seem to be successful, hopefully in a variety of contexts. Maguire does not wish to shun or reject the political arena on campus. Indeed, he realizes that this is the place in which reform must be initiated. He feels that change can best be accomplished in institutions that see their existence as a series of occasions which are full of potent, symbolic, and actual possibilities for change. In other words, the institution is perceived as growing and full of the potential of change. He also points out that change requires new alliances between constituencies, alliances which have perhaps not worked before. Moreover, change occurs in institutions in which there is a lively circulation both of new individuals and of changing perspectives among individuals.

Using these as fundamental change axioms, Maguire points out what logically follows: New change patterns should as much as possible be related to, not more emphatically differentiated from, already existing patterns. He recommends a careful step-by-step change process, securing each gain before attempting the next. It is also important to engage the interest and commitment of marginal individuals on the campus. He suggests that simply gathering information and doing research on the nature of the institution can be a very useful change device. Whenever possible the security of those persons uncertain as to the nature of the change should be increased; they should be made to feel a part of the process and should be given assurances that the new procedure will be evaluated to determine its effectiveness. Running through Maguire's analysis is the important belief that both those in favor of change and those who are reluctant to change are human beings with very characteristic human attributes. This is sometimes forgotten in our heated rhetoric.

Richard Wertz's fascinating account of the new curriculum at the Massachusetts Institute of Technology is a case study of how curricular change comes about. We place the chapter here in sequence because it follows nicely on Maguire's more general analysis.

MIT, which serves the military-industrial complex with such obvious success, was one of the first institutions to develop a program in social inquiry which suggested rather radical investigations of a number of phenomena one does not usually think of in connection with MIT. It is easy to see from Wertz's analysis how one thing led to another. Students and faculty worked together, and for the most part they followed Maguire's prescriptions. The crucial nature of the MIT sanctuary of the AWOL soldier perhaps indicates one prescription for change that Maguire did not mention: always capitalize on the unexpected event.

Perhaps the key to the strategies used by Wertz and his colleagues at MIT was to get the institution to become more self-conscious about what it was doing and why. This is one of the central principles of reform in higher education—pointing the analytical skills and techniques of higher education at the institution of higher education itself. The strategies and tactics used at MIT are a nice combination of those of the guerilla war expert and those of the classical military strategist. Both seem to be useful in their place. When one deals with the formal bureaucracy of the institution, one wishes to be as sincere and rational as possible, yet one also must give the impression that individuals who agree with the movement are everywhere, that they represent no particular interest, and that they are constantly shifting both ground and issues. It is possible, as Wertz's chapter points out, to adopt both styles at the same time.

The last chapter of Part Two is by Edward Schwartz, who argues cogently for a radical perspective leading toward a new kind of institution. It is clear from his opening comments that Schwartz was not pleased with the efforts of most of the rest of us. Pointing out with a great deal of justification the agony of many intellectual liberals, Schwartz believes that there is a new vision and that it belongs primarily to the young. His strategy for change involves making possible the creation of community between and within individuals who share in the new vision. It may begin with two people and expand to thousands. In the new university toward which he strives, everyone reads but out of a sense of interest rather than duty. Everyone teaches because everyone learns. It is a radical communiversity in which the loyalty within the community is primarily from those who agree with radical objectives. It is a reconstructionist university in that the institution will be used to change society along radical lines. The certifying role is clearly not a function of this new kind of institution. Schwartz sees the temporary university as pallid and unable to act on the commitments of individuals within it. He would like to see a communiversity full of activists who believe in using the institution to reform society. He points out that the denial of subjectivity and the interest in detached neutrality will lead us in the direction suggested in Callahan's chapter, in that we will be hopelessly imprisoned by the old Aristotelian notion that in any conflict both sides are partially right and thus no action is possible.

The crucial point of disagreement between Schwartz's chapter and the others is that many of the other authors feel that change must happen in a way consistent with the commitments, both moral and intellectual, of the institution. Schwartz is not sure that this is true. The ends justify the means, and when one takes on a tough adversary one must adopt tough strategies in order to defeat him. Using Columbia as a model, Schwartz points out how such a radical community can be built: beginning with an experimental college which will attract the specific interests of many students, working from there into a program of black studies and concern for black people and their problems, encouraging processes whereby students can criticize and challenge the institution, and expanding the nature of this new radical community to include more people who go out in classical guerilla style to infiltrate the ranks. By comparing Maguire's strategy for reform with Schwartz's and looking at the picture of MIT drawn by Wertz, we perhaps have come full circle on the available strategies for reform.

The chapters which end the book give us several ideas of where we may be going. For Paul Spike, the new experience is primarily a disillusionment with the methods and the "facts" of the present dominating cultural style. He sees little joy among his student colleagues. He feels that most of them are leading lives of quiet desperation in dealing with the war, with racial strife, and with ineffective and unmanageable political and economic structures. He points out perceptively that the cultural revolution which others see in the future may have passed already. We may simply have ignored it. He sees a generation gap in terms of the perceptual patterns of youth and adults.

Myron B. Bloy, author of the next chapter, believes that there is a counter-culture. Looking for a definition of this new vision, we find it in Bloy's sentence concerning those students who participated in civil rights demonstrations, particularly in the South. They discovered "that it was possible for their lives to be radically open to the lives of others, especially the dispossessed; and this, they began to realize, was what it meant to be authentically human." The new vision is, for Bloy, thoroughly consistent with the best of Christian principle and thus does not represent an amoral attempt to avoid the questions of religion. As he suggests, "the students have instinctively rediscovered the old spiritual and newer psychoanalytical axiom that self-love is a necessary condition for mature neighbor-love." He sees the new movement largely in student terms as being full of integrity and spiritual commitment. Like Schwartz, Bloy believes that one of the most exciting areas of expansion of consciousness in American life today is the black consciousness movement. Because of the distance of blacks from the dominant culture, because of their marginality to the systems of production and distribution, they have been able to develop a consistent life style which forms an alternative, says Bloy, to the dominant middle-class culture. To a far greater degree than Schwartz, Bloy feels that what has happened is "youth's recovery of the perception that man is made for love." Bloy gives only one page to a specific description of how universities would look if they were to incorporate more of the new consciousness into their activity, but what he says is important. The curriculum would clearly involve dancing as an important requirement along with freshman composition. Esalen techniques would be a regular part of the curriculum. One would also study more conventional things, but as models and inspirations for one's own expression, not just as objects for scholarly categorization.

We end with Lawrence C. Howard's creative expression of black consciousness and its relationship to higher education. Howard's chapter demands participation of the reader, and in its very form suggests a new style which makes one less a passive nonentity and more an individual whose response to the chapter will be unique. Howard's chapter invites all of us—black, white, rich, poor, student, faculty—to participate in the relationship between the counter-culture and the experience of being black in American contemporary society. Howard's central accusation rings clear: "The university has not demonstrated, by ideas or acts, its commitment to people." It is clear, also, that higher education produces some trained incapacities in that the more educated one is, the more difficult it is to see the deepest roots of the current crisis of identity. The problem, as Howard sees it, exists not only because of our new technology, but because of the myth of the machine as anti-human and deeply threatening to the forces of love and joy. This anti-human instrumentalism is carried forward by a vanguard of new mandarins who support the status quo and will to a large extent determine the future.

The black consciousness is opposed to this technetronic perspective. It is because blacks have lived on the edge of the technetronic revolution that they can see it in a more realistic way than others who are immersed in it every day of their lives. Black consciousness is open to whites as well. Howard says, "Blacks are people of any color who are consciously dedicated to emancipation, civil rights, shared interdependence, freedom for human fulfillment. The black priority is pro-people." Howard ends with some specific accounting of what a black-conscious university would be like. But to say more about the chapter at this stage would be to hinder one's ability to participate, which is a necessity.

The chapters in this book present some new thinking about the identity crisis in higher education, and they pull together some old thoughts in new ways. If one has grasped the possibility that not only do individuals lead lives of quiet desperation, but institutions and societies may do so as well, then perhaps the title of the book is merited. The identity crisis is not the unique province of the young; those over thirty—or whatever the current figure may be—also have deep and agonizing concerns as to the rightness of their actions and values. It is perhaps the open and trusting expression of these concerns that makes this book important to all of us.

PART

CHANGES IN INTELLECTUAL ORIENTATION

ONE

Daniel Callahan

Facts, Values, and Commitments

I

The distinction between the "descriptive" and the "normative," between "facts" and "values," is deeply imbedded in recent Western intellectual life. And it is, of course, enshrined in the American university. Its supposed utility is twofold. First, it is thought to represent a viable distinction inherent in the nature of things. Facts, roughly, are thought to be "the way things are," quite apart from, and metaphysically indifferent to, what people make of them or the valuation they assign them. Facts are just there and would be there even if there were no interested spectators to take account of them. Values, by contrast, are thought to be the creation of human beings: the worth they see in things or want to attribute to them.

Unlike facts, which have an independent bruteness, values are human artifacts, subjective in meaning and origin; we choose our values, but not our facts. Facts are outside us, while values are inside.

Second, the fact-value distinction is thought to have a valid institutional, political use. In a pluralistic society, and in its universities, basic disagreements and heated arguments are bound to occur. While civility and mutual tolerance are some help in keeping people from each other's throats, the fact-value distinction is even more serviceable. By means of this distinction it becomes possible, it is thought, to provide a solid ground for the coexistence of people with very different perspectives on life. All they must do is accept the fact-value distinction and scrupulously apply it in their professional-academic life. Thus they are to seek and tell the truth about facts, being carefully detached and impartial, always distinguishing between a fact and a value. If they want to espouse values, there is no particular objection so long as these values are openly and honestly labeled as such. With these as the academic ground rules, presumably, there will be a place for the common, relatively impersonal business of gathering new information and contributing to the advance of human knowledge, while at the same time leaving room for the more subjective, idiosyncratic business of forming and espousing values. Civil peace in the university is thereby made possible.

Behind this reasoning is the assumption that the university can create a neutral framework for the pursuit of facts and the espousal of value; most universities of any prestige believe they have already done so. The neutrality is supposedly guaranteed by canons of research and teaching which: do not commit the university to any particular ideology, set of facts, or theory of facts; allow unrestricted inquiry into any and all facts, subject only to the condition that inquirers conform to the accepted ethics and methodologies of their particular disciplines; open the door to all serious people, regardless of their personal values or backgrounds; and allow the expression of personal values so long as these do not interfere with "unbiased" teaching and research. On the face of it, there is nothing whatever objectionable about all this. Some, indeed many, people have flourished in this kind of atmosphere; they feel free, act in ways that would be accounted free, and add to the accumulation of human knowledge.

It is only when the neutrality of this framework is measured against the broader, nonacademic society as a whole that its inherent biases begin to manifest themselves. The predominance of one race (white) and of one class (middle) means that the facts sought are those which interest that race and class; the facts which would interest those not represented are scanted. Moreover, the values espoused are values which contribute to the welfare of the dominant group. What has become clear, as new clientele are admitted to the universities, is that the old neutrality was geared to favor the interests and latent values of the old clientele. What the new groups see is that the neutrality not only scanted things which should be explored within the university itself, but also forestalled any possibility of the university bringing about substantive changes in the society. For universities are owned by that society, depend upon that society for their prestige, and admit within the sphere of neutrality only what the society will tolerate under the rubric of free speech and investigation. In addition, there is a built-in bias to the neutrality by virtue of the dominant place of the older, non-student members of the university community: administrators, faculty, and trustees. They are the ones who define responsible work and research; they say what is fair and unfair. They establish the limits to which personal values may be espoused and acted out. By proclaiming that neutrality on the institutional level is glorious, even in the face of great social evils, they lend credence to the notion that human beings can be neutral, detached, and value-free without harming society as a whole. In a society which systematically evades its social responsibilities, the existence of important institutions which are neutral merely encourages individuals to be neutral—which usually means ignoring the problems.

That the fact-value distinction has lingered on in the universities is traceable to three sources: a general ignorance of the devastating criticisms which have been leveled at its theoretical validity; the failure to discover a suitable alternative which would have the same kind of institutional and political values as the old distinction; and the absence of powerful pressure groups sufficiently strong to overcome the distinction at either the theoretical or practical level.

Had enough people in the universities been informed about the theoretical dubiety of the fact-value distinction it would have tottered long ago. I will mention here only a few of the critiques calling it into question. In the natural sciences, it has long been known that explanatory theories are human constructs. Theories are devised for the sake of achieving some goal sought by the investigator; the language (mathematical, pictorial, or verbal) of the theory is also a construct, a human invention; the results of "empirical" investigation will depend almost exclusively on the inventive genius of the theory and its attendant language; what is a fact or a law will be only a function of the theory. The whole process is shot through with human goals and values, human language and concepts. Subjectivity is rampant in even the most hard-nosed empirical discipline, the natural sciences. And what is true there is also true in the biological sciences (see Michael Polanyi's *Personal Knowledge*) and in the social sciences.[1]

As W. V. Quine has pointed out, speaking of recent philosophical thought:

> *There is a tendency . . . to think of facts as concrete. This is fostered by the commonplace ring of the word and the hint of bruteness. . . . Yet what can they be, and be concrete? The sentences "Fifth Avenue is six miles long" and "Fifth Avenue is a hundred feet wide," if we suppose them true, presumably state different facts, yet the only concrete or at any rate physical object involved is Fifth Avenue. . . . Our two sentences last quoted are true because of Fifth Avenue, . . . because it was planned and made that way, and because of the way we use our words.*[2]

[1] See especially M. Polanyi, *Personal Knowledge* (New York: Harper Torchbooks, 1964) and M. Grene, *The Knower and the Known* (New York: Basic Books, 1966).

[2] W. V. O. Quine, *Word and Object* (New York: Wiley, 1960), p. 247.

On another front in philosophy, the supposed distinction between *is* and *ought* and the supposed underivability of the latter from the former (the "naturalistic fallacy") has come in for increasing criticism (for example, by Henry D. Aiken).[3] More broadly, it has been recognized of late that what someone chooses to work on in the first place (the facts that interest him) reflects certain valuations and orientations, and that the discovery of certain facts carries with it major social consequences (for example, DNA and the genetic code).

Even if all these trends (related to and a major rationale behind the sociology of knowledge) were recognized, however, we might still lack a basis for a good consensus, particularly of the institutional-political sort. One possible alternative, it seems to me, is sheer illusion: that every professor, say, be free to express his own values as vigorously as possible, just so long as he so labels them as his values and is fair to other positions. Yet insofar as this proposal keeps alive the fact-value distinction, or presupposes it, the old error is perpetuated. In addition, what is considered fair will be (usually) nothing more than a reflection of local mores. Twenty years ago it was not considered unfair for secular philosophy departments to all but ignore medieval philosophy; it was felt that this philosophy was not respectable enough to be subject to the norm of fairness, or that, having been examined, it has "fairly" been rejected. Twenty years ago it was not felt unfair that the American Negro received short shrift in American history courses; it was believed that there was not enough Negro history of merit to be dealt with or acknowledged. A basis for procedural consensus is needed, but the fact-value distinction does not provide it.

The absence of powerful pressure groups capable of overcoming, at both the theoretical and practical levels, the tenuous fact-value distinction was a mark of American university life until very recently. The universities were controlled by, intended for, and staffed by white middle-class Americans of generally Protestant origins. In this kind of university culture it was almost impossible to see the value commitments lurking behind "objective" scholarship

[3] H. D. Aiken, *Reason and Conduct* (New York: Knopf, 1962), pp. 44ff.

and research. There were, to return to my earlier examples, too few Catholics around to scream about the kind of "fairness" which confidently dismissed medieval philosophy and too few Negroes to howl about the absence of Negro history. Moreover, as long as the social interests of the universities—their class and clientele—coincided with those of white, middle-class America, there were present no forces even to make it dawn upon the universities that they did represent a certain value system. The most subtle danger of the fact-value distinction is that it provides an easy way for those who pride themselves on being honest and open to delude themselves. They may be well enough aware of some of their values, but, if the social atmosphere is homogeneous, they are likely to be persuaded by that atmosphere that certain commonly accepted values are not values at all but only facts. One of the really crucial contributions of the sociology of knowledge is its insight that what a society, or group, decides to call fact will be a direct consequence of its value system. For a racist society, it is not just a belief that Negroes are inferior, it is taken to be a fact; the homogeneity of the racist viewpoint is such that those who share it come to think it a description of the way things are. (There is, in this respect, no more insidious an intellectual notion than that of "telling it like it is," for "like it is" will depend upon the perspective of the one doing the telling.)

Fortunately, there now exist enough dissenters, out-groups, and despised minorities on most campuses to put some pressure on the local and national version of the facts. Nothing, socially speaking, will more rapidly tend to break down the fact-value distinction than the existence of groups who have different facts, or who interpret the same facts in different ways.

Yet to talk of the importance of breaking down the fact-value distinction raises a number of problems. If it can be agreed that the distinction has been overdrawn, and that its demise as a sacred cow would be salutary, is this to say that there are no facts, only values? Obviously one should be wary of going that far. Short of solipsistic idealism as a philosophical stance, most people believe that, in some sense, there does exist a reality outside themselves. There *is* a bruteness to reality; people, things, and events impinge upon our body and our consciousness. The careful philosopher may want to point out that the "law of gravity" represents a scientific construct and also to note that the fact of gravity is an empirical truth, that is, a truth forever contingent upon the possibility, however remote, that an exception to the law could be discovered. Which is only to say it is not a logical contradiction to deny the law of gravity. But distinctions of this kind are not meant to imply that it is safe to stand in the path of an avalanche or to jump from high places. A person who said he was going to leap from the top of the Empire State Building, arguing that the law of gravity is just the creation of scientists, would be a fool, however correct his discernment that the law is a construct. Ordinary sanity requires that we take account of reality, however much we may quibble about the exact interpretation of that reality. And it is this ordinary sanity which gives any talk of facts a persistent plausibility. If we mean by a fact some particular or general quality of bruteness, of reality external to our consciousness, then we are on relatively safe ground.

Yet this perception requires also the complementary perception (given us by the sociology of knowledge, as well as by what is known about the construction of scientific theory) that human beings are able to manipulate facts (for example, change the environment, turn iron ore into steel, and so on), to take different stances toward the same facts (for example, a tree can be looked upon as a thing of beauty, as a windbreak, as a source of wood to build houses, or as something for children to climb in), and to make some decisions about which facts are important and which are not, to choose among, and select, the available facts according to our goals and interests.

None of these human capacities implies that reality is simply a figment of the subjective self, nor do they deny the bruteness of reality. They only imply the plasticity of reality, expressed in the possibility of manipulating reality and of successfully taking different stances toward it. Thus facts may be said to exist "out there," regardless of our values, as long as it is also said that the existent facts are subject to human explanations and human uses. There are, of course, limits to the plasticity of reality, but even these limits are more often than not still unknown (that much at least the progress of modern science has demonstrated), subject to a potential human ability to transcend them. This is only to say that the facts are rarely fixed and permanent, and the source of their plasticity is the human subject who interacts with them, interpreting, using, manipulating, defining them.

Seen in this light, the fact-value distinction ceases to denote a sharp dichotomy in the nature of things, but instead reveals itself as a dialectical relationship between subject and object, self and non-self, man and nature, creator and created. It is a relationship resistant to fixed boundaries and full of surprises. A painting is a fact, a material object "out there" (hanging on a wall), but this fact came into existence because of an exercise of values (the belief of the artist that it was good to paint the picture). A city is a fact also, but it represents the value choice that urban life is preferable to rural life; had many people not made this choice the fact of urbanization would not exist. Yet once the city exists, the facts of life in the city will help shape values (for example, desired family size, educational aspirations, prized styles of life). Values create facts and facts create values.

Closely related to the fact-value distinction are a number of other dichotomies, equally in need of being placed in a more dialectical relationship. Three can be mentioned: thought-action; analysis-intervention; thinking-feeling. Under the neutrality model of the university, it is essentially a place of thought and analysis. The notion of the university as a marketplace of ideas, the key to the liberal defense of academic freedom, presupposes that the main business of the university centers on the mind. But what of the rest of the body and what of the practical implications of ideas? Minds do not exist independently of bodies. That trivial observation has serious implications. At the most primitive level, it is not just minds which create or analyze ideas. It is human beings who do so; the ideas which interest them, those they choose to analyze, the methods of analysis chosen, will all reflect personal and social histories. Ideas do not exist apart from human beings and can with only minimal profit be analyzed independently of their personal and social context. Drives, emotions, feelings, overt or covert social pressures all have their influence. Any analysis of ideas which ignores this human context will, in its understanding of the ideas, be truncated and misleading. Any analysis which proceeds as if the affective life of those doing the analysis can be ignored runs the risk of bias or blindness. Even to carry out the project of analysis, then, feelings have to be taken into account; the notion of neutral minds in neutral institutions analyzing ideas in a neutral way is a myth that can only be sustained by presuming minds without bodies.

If analysis cannot proceed apart from a human context, there is still the larger question of whether analysis is enough anyway. What is one to do with the results of thought and analysis? What will others do with the results? What ought, could, or should be done with the results? These are pertinent questions, not only because students ask them, but because history shows that ideas are used and not just thought about; theories are applied as well as created. What the universities have tried to do is to leave the application and practical implications of ideas to those outside the university. By narrowing the range of academic responsibility to thinking, analyzing, and researching, but not doing, the way has been left open to a misuse of ideas and knowledge. It is a splendid testimony to the scientific conscience that the nuclear scientists themselves took the lead, after World War II, in calling attention to the moral dimension of atomic research. It would have been an even more splendid testimony had this same community restrained and criticized itself during the war—before it had created nuclear weapons, the use of which was immediately taken out of its hands. These points are not lost on students. Professors who work on military research projects are not just doing pure research in a neutral vein; they are doing research which, when the results are used, can change —and often extinguish—human life.

But it is not only a question of perceiving that ideas have consequences and that those who deal in ideas bear responsibility for them. There also comes a point when analysis puts before people the responsibility to act on what they have learned. Those who know the data on poverty cannot stop once they have done the academic work of collecting and analyzing the data; it has then to be called to the attention of those who do not know the data— moral conclusions should be drawn and then pressed upon the people and upon the government. This means, of course, controversy, a loss of neutrality. But anything less is inhuman. A social division of labor which allots to academicians the accumulation of knowledge and to politicians the dissemination or application of it has disastrous consequences. The former are confirmed in their self-serving view that the quality of life in society is "outside their discipline." The latter, assuming they even know of the available knowledge, are confirmed in their view that they may do as they see fit with the knowledge made available to them (ignoring it altogether if they choose). Only when it is recognized, on purely human grounds, that those who analyze may and often will have to intervene to see that the work makes a difference—being used and not misused—can there be the possibility of morally responsible research and a morally responsible place for the university in society.

The distinction between thinking and feeling, inadequate enough even when the aim is pure analysis, is all the more deficient when the ends of education come into view. College catalogues have always prated on about developing "the whole man," which usually meant that the college had an athletic program, religious clubs, and extracurricular political organizations. But what went on in the classroom was, and in most places still is, essentially a rationalistic business: students are taught how to think, and thinking, for most people, means learning how to put aside feelings, personality, and bias for a pure contemplation or analysis of the thing-in-itself. Yet it is self-evident that this cannot and probably should not ever be done. The motivation to learn in the first place does not result from becoming convinced by arguments in favor of learning; it is a process of becoming humanly involved with other selves and with the world. Questions then arise which need answers; the questions pull people forward. People feel when they think; what they think will usually be a consequence of those things they feel strongly about, what has intrigued them, captured their imagination, stimulated them. And people think when they feel; what they feel will be a consequence of the ideas they entertain, the experiences they have opened themselves to, and the perception of where ideas lead.

The "whole man" is not a bad notion, but there will be no such man unless the relationship between thought, feeling, action, and intervention is rich and dialectical, not compartmentalized and departmentalized. A student who has learned how to feel and to perceive has learned something. His education cannot stop when his head has been stuffed with ideas duly analyzed; it is only beginning at that point.

How can this full range of dialectical relationships be reflected in the life of the university? First, any mode of education which simply sets before students some supposed body of knowledge or facts would be inadmissible. A student should from the outset be allowed to explore the role of value systems in the designation and creation of facts. This would mean an interrogation of the concept of reality and an analysis of the role of human beings in defining, classifying, constructing, and using reality. Inevitably, if this is done well, the dialectical relationship between facts and values will quickly manifest itself; and thus would the role of man as creator and definer of facts come to the fore.

Second, a scrupulous regard for the fact-value distinction could no longer serve as a test of a teacher's integrity, teaching ability, or scholarly talents. If the university is conceived of as a place which aspires to more than the role of discoverer, cataloguer, and retailer of hard facts, then those whose self-chosen vocation is the creation of values would have as honored a place as anyone else. A teacher who published nothing but spent his time in community organization, passing on his experience to students, would be as eligible for promotion, honors, and student attention as anyone else; he would be a creator of values, an honorable academic goal. A student who chose to spend his time painting, or writing, or organizing would, in a similar way, be considered a good student; he would also be spending his time creating value. In the cases of both teacher and student, one who wanted to change reality would be as important to the academic community as one who simply wanted to discover and label the facts of reality. In the past, praise and good grades went to the latter rather than the former. Yet both can have a place, depending upon personal talents and dispositions. Moreover, it will usually turn out that the person who tries to do either one thing or the other well will be forced to take account of the dialectic. To create a new reality usually requires that one learn something about the old reality; he may have to amass in his mind some outdated, dull facts before he can create new ones. Once the dialectic is seen, it will also be seen that it tends to be self-corrective, dealing out nasty blows to those who think they can live within the exclusive boundaries of one or the other of its poles (facts or values).

Third, a recognition of the dialectic can help clarify the relationship of the university to the community. A major source of hypocrisy in the university is its Janus-faced relationship to the outside community. When it is under attack by the community it takes refuge in the rhetoric of academic freedom, claiming it is just a marketplace of ideas, all of which must be freely explored; in the same breath, it denies that its purpose is to subvert or change the community. When it wants money from the community, however, it makes a different claim. Then it talks of the university's service to the community, the good it does for the community, the goods it produces for the community. The last thing it would admit during these moments is that it is merely a marketplace of ideas, with no effect on the community. The university as money-raiser is the university as self-proclaimed public servant, utterly engrossed in the life of the community. Under the dialectic, the tension and hypocrisy would come to an end. For, at its richest, the university is both a marketplace of ideas and a public servant. It serves the community by existing as a place where facts are discovered and ideas debated. It also serves when it acts as a place which tries to create values for the community and change those facts in the community which need changing.

A number of problems remain. Even if it is granted that the fact-value distinction as a rigid dichotomy can no longer stand, one might admit that it provided at least some criteria for achieving a procedural consensus and impartial norms for judging faculty members. What can be put in its place? I do not believe that anything specific need be substituted. The questions to be asked of the work of a teacher-scholar are not whether he observes the fact-value distinction but whether he has regard for the work and talent of others, respecting their rights and their needs; whether he is making some contribution to the academic community or the outside community, or both; and whether what he does with his students is of some use in their lives. Under the old fact-value distinction, values were often smuggled in under the name of fact, so that the distinction provided an illusory basis for a procedural consensus. One may have to accept the possibility that there will be no simple norms by which to judge a man's work. Whatever norms are developed will be a function of what particular academic communities are trying to do, the kinds of students they have, and the special strengths and interests of particular faculty members.

One result of vagueness of criteria is to bring to the surface a salient element of any working, viable academic community: it should be a place where values contend with each other. Often enough it has been, but because the value commitments were below the surface, hidden by a facade of objectivity, they were never allowed the possibility of a fruitful clash; worse still, those in a position to define objectivity (those with power) were able to impose values, and do so in the name of truth and free investigation. Not only was the university the loser, but the student lost as well. To be sure, an open struggle between competing value claims could have its unpleasant side, but this danger seems unavoidable. The only alternative is to allow one group the unrestricted right to make value decisions affecting the whole community; the danger of this kind of procedure, however peaceful it might be, need not be underscored.

Is there any way of testing the value of the approach outlined in this chapter? In one sense, no. The problem of the fact-value distinction is in great part a metaphysical and epistemological problem. Obviously it needs to be discussed at much greater length than I have been able to do here. But even if a new relationship between facts and values could be worked out, say along the dialectical lines I have sketched, it could take years to permeate the American academic scene. And it would take even longer for its value to be tested in practice. For the purpose of a more rapid testing, only the use of experimental colleges, or venturesome divisions within more traditional universities, is likely to suffice.

At least three experiments would be necessary. The first would be the structuring of a curriculum which would begin the educational process with courses and educational experiences designed to bring home the way in which human beings construct facts and values. Courses in the sociology of knowledge, in theory construction, and in critical philosophical analysis would be important, as would historical investigations of the way in which earlier cultures and communities tried to create worlds of meaning and value. The second experiment would be a formal commitment on the part of a college to use the creation of value, rather than simply academic publishing, as a norm for the hiring and retaining of faculty members. Thus it could be made clear that the standards for promotion, salary, and the like are multiple, making especially clear that work in the outside community counts for as much as more traditional kinds of academic productivity. The third would be a formal commitment on the part of a college to support those students who choose to make their college career an occasion for the creation of value. This would mean specifying a variety of approaches a student might take in order to satisfy any degree requirement. He would be free to choose a traditional approach, stressing formal courses and the amassing of knowledge; or free to choose an activist approach, involving very little course work but very much in the way of community service work; or free to choose a creative approach, that is, an approach suitable for those who wanted to write, or paint, or compose music.

Just as it is now possible to satisfy degree requirements by taking a variety of different courses, and choosing different kinds of majors, far greater variety would be added by allowing basic choices among styles of undergraduate life; students could choose a traditional scholarly style, or an activist style, or an esthetically creative style (or any other style that might seem valuable). Each of these styles would entail different kinds of requirements, and their formalization would be the work of those familiar with different styles of life; a professor of Elizabethan literature is not usually well equipped to judge what one needs to be an effective community organizer. Even here, though, it ought to be open, in some reasonably formal way, for those engrossed in one style of life to press the claims of that style and to resist any educational process which too early preempted a student.

Ruel W. Tyson, Jr.

Confusions of Culture

II

Sometimes reflections before revolutions are subversive; often reflection during revolution is a necessity. If the present situation is revolutionary, there is a poverty of names with which to grasp its parts and its history. The traditions which inform university life are in major ways the sources of this perplexity; that reexamination of some of the cultural movements embodied in university traditions can create resources for responding to present necessities remains a steady hope for those who value these traditions more in their potential reformulations than in their past achievements.

The obstacles to reexamination, even in a period of revolution and reaction, are formidable. The resistance to action uninformed by critical reassessment of the university's traditions is much less forbidding—and much more dangerous. If the causes and meanings of revolution are not misplaced in a "crisis," it is possible —but surpassingly difficult—to seek a new definition of the situation. The search is a high-risk enterprise in description and speculation.

Eccentric contortions are the gestures of a man trying to know where he stands. The procurators of categorical neatness flee in despair, and by their flight they send an important message: the inherited traditions of discourse, the operative classifications of knowledge, and the social arrangements through which these divisions of the university's work are both mediated and legitimated are all formidable objects for reexamination. Official definitions of the present situation are embodied in university culture and organization and are among the strongest elements of resistance to a new definition of the situation. The necessities of the contemporary situation demand an inventory of resistance to any attempt to find new balance.

Men in stress are frequently as prodigal in their responses to discontent as they are clever in their neglect of history on behalf of normalcy. Sometimes the interruption of contentment inspires a yearning for restoration that is indeed heroic. Much effort is consumed in plotting a story and in achieving its enactment in order to satisfy yearnings for restoration. But the search for restoration is a refusal to live in the ambiguities of a history unforeseen by institutional scanning devices.

Here is the plot of a rather old story: Things were going as a matter of course. Then there was a crisis, or a disruption; next began a search for a pattern that would be like the former routine. This story has a long beginning, a brief, perhaps dramatic, middle, and an end that depicts the future by extrapolating the pattern of the pre-crisis past. As the characters in this story move into a future presumed to be familiar to them, individual and institutional techniques of forgetting are practiced upon the memories and messages of the crisis. As these memories pass into official oblivion they take with them any potential lessons for a future different from the received, if recently disturbed, past. The uncertainties of reflection, and hence the possibilities for new actions, are surrendered for the certainties of forgetting and remembering. Essays in speculation and description concerning the causes, conflicts, changes, and meanings of the advents of history receive little institutional, if much private, attention. Deviance from the norm is thereby exorcised. Recollections of the normative past are intensified. There is studied neglect of the wisdom latent in the foolishness of history. This cycle is one response to manifestations of discontent in the universities.

To sketch the plot in so primitive a fashion is not to award proper respect to the politics of selective recollection and forgetting. The refusal to inquire into the meanings of contemporary history, in so far as these meanings may be knowable inside the university, expresses powerful attachments to received cultural and institutional forms, attachments which certain segments of the university perpetuate in their choice of candidates who are to become certified colleagues in these forms. No human groups, even institutions where men and women spend their days inquiring into the origins of matter and into the revolutions of the past, appear to be exempt from selective forgetting and remembering.

However, as long as there is a plurality of human groups and as long as representatives of these groups have access to public space and public media, alternate proposals for response to the present discontents can be made. In spite of the growth of literature on "the crisis in the universities," there is still a poverty of description and speculation about the complex ways in which the received social structures and the academic cultures they support combine to create the present confusions in the universities. (Current literature on the university question offers an excellent opportunity to study how the intellectual traditions perpetuated by the universities are played back to the universities in commentary and criticism. What impresses a reader of this growing body of work is that the categorical commitments of these commentators and critics frequently lead them to reduce the independent status of thought and criticism to epiphenomena, that is, to expressions of other forces, such as psychological drives or power relations.)

There are other stories to try out on the future; there are other responses to the present. If such explorations are to be helpful, they must be accompanied by more exigent attention to the intellectual inheritance modern universities tacitly and hence uncritically transmit through their rites and manners and through their curricular structures.

However, these new readings of things assumed to be familiar cannot be achieved if the usual disciplinary borders are to be respected; disciplinary borders are instances of neatness akin to the categorical neatness of the internal structures of academic disciplines. For example, the divisions between intellectual history and the history and sociology of institutions need to be transcended.[1] This need is especially acute when the university itself is the subject of study. And since the university has sponsored these divisions of knowledge in its institutional organization, it is in the university setting that disciplinary transcendence is most difficult to obtain.

That the present state of the university requires attentive disrespect for the segregation of inquiries that characterizes the way knowledge is organized and nurtured in the university is obvious to some and entirely obscure to many. A modest hope is that all will find the issue openly debatable. But here a certain risk intrudes, as Walter Bagehot observed: "A government by discussion, if it can be born, at once breaks down the yoke of fixed custom. The idea of the two is inconsistent."[2]

One element in the current disorders is the inconsistency between customary structures within the university and the revolutionary impact of discoveries in diverse fields of inquiry. The ideals of the Enlightenment continue to be practiced in the university, but they are increasingly pursued in conservative forms of order. The institutionalization of Enlightenment values in the university has produced its own yoke of custom—an irony of history because custom, tradition, and prejudice were the enemies of the eighteenth-century Enlightenment. Only if the structures which inform and order the search for knowledge are critically reordered can

[1] See, for example, J. G. A. Pocock, "The History of Political Thought: A Methodological Enquiry," *Philosophy, Politics, and Society* (Second Series), ed. P. Laslett and W. G. Runciman (Oxford: Blackwell, 1962), pp. 183–202.

[2] W. Bagehot, *Physics and Politics* (Boston: Beacon Press, 1956), p. 117.

there be addresses to the present situation that encourage openness toward the problems of history—and thereby some hope for creative responses—instead of reparations that refine existing techniques for disregarding history and for the restoration of the pre-crisis version of the past.

It is, of course, misleading to speak of changing structures as if "structures" were not a short term for how persons order their relations with each other by the assignment and assumption of roles and by other means. To speak of changing structures is to speak of changing the attachments persons have to the forms in which they perform their work. Ultimately, it is to speak of transforming the basic self-images of persons in relation to their work; in the case of the university we refer to the social and civil setting of intellectual action and the cognitive maps of knowledge pursued within this setting. These are the dimensions of personal involvement which incline people to resist exposure to the disturbances of history, rather than to reflect upon them for disclosures of any portents they may hold for other responses.

Perhaps an irony of unspecified proportions is in the making. Perhaps we know more than we can tell.[3] Telling is difficult because the structures within the university system which have expedited our knowing discourage telling what we know and what we know about the social and intellectual conditions of knowing. Telling is an essential element in collective action that aspires to be reasonable; mutual action among the constituents of the university will be the final test of the quality of their response to the present discontent.

The contemporary university abundantly fulfills the dreams of the Enlightenment. Earlier visions have become concrete in building and machine, formula and profession, prestige and wealth. The clerks now have International Travel Cards. Voltaire, feted by kings and entertained by queens, would have much to learn from contemporary adepts at grantsmanship. Knowledge has become industry and gross national product. The Enlightenment has come of

[3] See M. Polanyi, *The Tacit Dimension* (Garden City, N.Y.: Doubleday Anchor, 1967), Chapter One.

age. It has retired former tutors.[4] The university is the major context of its daily celebrations.

The premise of these celebrations supports the work and life of universities and research establishments. The premise is assumed by liberals and conservatives alike, though they may disagree over priorities in policy and over strategic and tactical devices. Comprehensive in import yet simple in statement, the premise is that knowledge is good; that lives invested in its pursuit are healthy; that the prestige accorded to knowledge and to its practitioners is productive of the common good; that the exercise of cognitive powers—the stern measures of word and number—in the discovery, transferal, and revision of knowledge is good for the person, society, and future generations. Knowledge and the good life are inconceivable without each other.

Should anyone risk the embarrassment of asking whether it is for the common good that the truth about everything be known, he would find that an affirmative is given tacitly every day in universities and research institutes. Socrates, when he was asked this question, replied in the affirmative. The lack of criticism of the governance of knowledge, the absence of discussion on this critical issue, perhaps would elicit a different response from Socrates.

The contemporary university is fully in possession of the heritage of Greek and Renaissance rationalism and, most especially, the rationalism of the eighteenth-century Enlightenment. It has become a commonplace description of how many people spend their workdays and analyze their dream work. It is less a commonplace to observe, however, that the practice of knowledge creates a mode of life of its own, generates typical cognitive patterns, orders its own kind of inclusive sensibility, and nurtures certain forms of the imagination. (The contemporary imagination is less and less informed by knowledge of history, understood as actions and events of an irrevocable character. Instead, technology and psychology nurture the modern imagination.) The practice of knowledge creates a morality of knowledge[5] and a way of life whose obviousness makes

[4] I. Kant, "What is Enlightenment?" (1784), in *On History*, edited and translated by L. W. Beck (Indianapolis: Bobbs, Merrill, 1963), pp. 3–10.

[5] "The Morality of Knowledge" is the working title of one of my

it difficult to discuss, whose wide acceptance makes it folly to question.

There are important exceptions to these observations. The Enlightenment, as its values are mediated through contemporary universities, is being reassessed. For some the Enlightenment is dead. Others are making up their minds about its status and its imperatives. Still others, in less than typical academic ways, are asking a question Rousseau was foolish or courageous enough to address to a learned academy of his day: "Has the restoration of the arts and sciences had a purifying effect upon morals?"[6] Perhaps because the precedents are unknown to them, many younger members of the university community are reinstating a tradition of inquiry about the morality of Enlightenment rationalism and its accompanying personal, political, and social consequences.

Frequently the methods of inquiry employed by the new critics of the Enlightenment would not be recognized as legitimate methods by academic traditionalists. We might also question the degree of self-consciousness in criticism of the Enlightenment. It is not clear that, as post-Enlightenment persons possessing the Enlightenment prejudice against traditions, the new critics know that it is the Enlightenment they are attacking.

The university is the arena for the forces of the mature Enlightenment and the counterforces that are attacking its commitment to "cognitive rationality"[7] and the policy formations and administrative arrangements which facilitate commitments to "cogni-

---

works, now in progress. I have recently discovered that the phrase was used by Erich Heller as a subtitle to an essay, "Faust's Damnation: The Morality of Knowledge," in *The Artist's Journey into the Interior and Other Essays* (New York: Random House, 1965). Heller's discussion of Nietzsche as "the first moralist of knowledge" (pp. 184ff.) is important. In an earlier unpublished paper on drug use in universities I employed the terms *ethics of scholarly asceticism* and *the ethics of ecstasy;* the former of these terms derives from Nietzsche's *The Genealogy of Morals,* his prime critique of the morality of knowledge. See also *Thus Spoke Zarathustra,* Second Part: "On the Land of Education," "On Immaculate Perception," and "On Scholars."

[6] J.-J. Rousseau, *The Social Contract and Other Discourses,* G. D. H. Cole (Ed.) (London: J. M. Dent, 1955), pp. 117–142.

[7] T. Parsons, "The Academic System: A Sociologist's View," *The Public Interest,* 1968, *13,* 173–197.

tive rationality." Courses, disciplines, majors, methodologies, curricula, the rhetorics of scholarly discourse, and the ordering of educational space and time are the policy formations made under the reigning conception of knowledge. It is plain that the values of academic culture, with its Enlightenment inheritance, cannot be separated from the administration of academic institutions, a fact which both educational reformers and critics of current concepts of knowledge need to remember. James S. Ackerman offers a telling example of conceptions of knowledge and the curriculum which serve as the policy formations expressing conceptions of knowledge:

> *Furthermore, the prevailing* scientia *not only may be hostile to images different from those it promotes, but consciously or unconsciously it may organize its education so that criticism is frustrated. This deficiency would explain some of the paradoxes of contemporary higher education, which, in being designed to promote empiricism and technological specialization, incidentally manages to stifle philosophical synthesis and ethical speculation. In proceeding from a broad survey at the base to a narrow parochialism at the apex, the university curriculum not only trains efficient specialists. It also protects obsolete scientism from being subjected to effective criticism by obstructing from the advanced student a commanding view of the topography of his culture.*[8]

If the central university system is the scene of daily celebrations of the Enlightenment, there are counter-festivals, on the periphery, in which a death watch is being kept over the achievements of the Enlightenment and its custodians. The death watch is festive since the destruction of the Enlightenment is anticipated as a liberation. It may in fact prove to be not a liberation, but a return to a tribal bondage, a Dionysian night. To say farewell to the Enlightenment may be imagined as an escape from rationalism in architecture, in ethics and esthetics, and in the dramaturgy of teaching and learning—an order of historical existence in which students and academicians receive powerful formations.

[8] J. S. Ackerman, "On Scientia," *Daedalus,* 1965, *94*(1), 22.

But will the departure from this inheritance become a return to a very old and dark place known in dream and prehistory? If there is to be death for the gods of light and line, are there some unnamed dark gods to embrace? Will we fall into terrible primordial diffusions and into unanticipated costs demanded by the disciplines of ecstasy if we flee from distance and ascetic discipline—from "the rational attitude" in knowledge and educational administration? Aron says:

Measurement—of working hours or output—is basic to that form of procedure which used to be termed capitalist, but is now recognised as being characteristic of all modern societies. Measurement leads to the endeavor to produce more in the same time, or to spend less time on producing the same amount, or to produce a more valuable output in less time. But to achieve this ambition quantitatively, it is also necessary to replace the usual methods of work and organization by reflection or calculation, that is, to adopt what Max Weber calls a "rational attitude," or what is also known as rationalization. Quantitative rationalization involves a new approach to the past and the future. The past, as such, is no longer respectable or sacred. The future is no longer looked upon as a repetition of what has gone before or as something inescapable. Tradition is no longer enough to ratify authority or institutions and, encouraged by success, men are determined to work out in advance those quantitative factors determining their future, such as the size of a given population, the resources at its disposal, and its living standards. Modern societies are the first ever to justify themselves by their future, the first in which the motto: "Man is the future of man," appears not so much blasphemous as commonplace.[9]

The term *youth culture* has more allusive than descriptive power. It is often used to suggest a vital "counter-culture."[10] There

[9] R. Aron, "The Epoch of Universal Technology," Encounter Pamphlet No. 1, *Encounter Magazine,* 1964, 4.

[10] T. Roszak, *The Making of a Counter Culture* (Garden City, N.Y.: Anchor, 1969). Also see M. Bloy, "Culture and Counter-Culture," *Commonweal,* 1969, *89,* 493–496.

is no doubt that attention should be paid to the groups and to the sensibilities of groups loosely clustered in a youth counter-culture. But it would be a mistake to identify students, even in metropolitan universities, with this counter-culture, though they do express many of the features and participate in many of the cultural forms of the counter-culture. The cultural forces that are represented by, or assumed in, the term *counter-culture* or *youth culture* have far deeper roots in history and a far wider circumference in social space than certain groups of cosmopolitan students or youth.

There is little doubt that this society is currently in a cultural revolution and that such terms as *youth culture* or *counter-culture* refer to that revolution within and without the university. The term *revolution,* however, is ambiguous. It can mean a total or radical change, a decisive shift in orientation. But it can also mean a repetition or rotation, a return, a replay, if not an instant replay.

Does contemporary youth culture as a counter-culture represent a creative advance, a new vision, or is it a regressive reaction by one major cultural inheritance against another major cultural inheritance which was its original enemy? The question can be expressed in another way: Is youth culture—by no means restricted to youth—a latter-day resurgence of romanticism or neoromanticism against its old enemy and counter-player, the Enlightenment? Are society in general and the universities in particular the scene of a return match between the clerks and the men of feeling?

A response to this question from representatives of the cultural revolution or aspirants for the new vision would be surprising. For these representatives would reject at least one major premise of the question, namely, that the past is worthy of attention, that history and tradition provide meaningful approaches to the understanding of the present. Their attitudes do not include recognition of pastness as a part of the present. Ministrations out of several pasts are not normative for the counter-culture. The only exception to this statement is the recognition of the past as negative, an obstacle.

The traditional enemy of the romantic sensibility, the man of rational attitude, likewise views the past as surpassed without continuation into the present and future.[11] Therefore, if the latter-day descendants of the *philosophes* were asked this question, they would have reservations about a major premise, for their historical progressivism would make it repugnant to them to admit that history has replays. Perhaps the qualification *counter* is an unfortunate prefix to *counter-culture* from the view of each of the presumed antagonists. Advocates of the counter-culture do not see the cultural revolution as a repetition or a return to an earlier engagement, much less as the continuation of the long engagement between romanticism and Enlightenment. Cultural revolution here means radically new orientations, new visions, and anticipations of their embodiments in the main institutional systems of the society, especially in the universities. There must be a politics of the cultural revolution if social structures supporting and ordering the values of the new vision are to be realized near the center of society rather than on its periphery.

The politics of the new vision will determine whether the new cultural values and new human sensibilities foreseen in the counter-culture are capable of political embodiment in a revised or new set of social structures. The politics of the new vision will test the community-founding sources of the counter-culture. The politics of the new culture will determine whether it is a minority culture, a dependent culture, or indeed a counter-culture in relation to the dominant culture. Will the politics of the new culture be in accord with its values?

Such a question cannot be resolved yet, but it is important that it be asked by those who live and work in universities. For in these institutions the conflict between the politics of scholarly asceticism—the values of cognitive rationality—and the politics of the new cultural sensibilities will be waged; indeed, the conflicts and negotiations are already under way. By examining this conflict, a number of plots for the future can be devised. It will also be possible to develop a more accurate description of our present historical situation. In addition, some preliminary determinations can be made on a larger question which is related to the previous query

[11] Aron, *loc. cit.*

about the possibility of a return match between the clerks of the Enlightenment and the men called romantics. That question is whether the post-Enlightenment critique of the Enlightenment—the cultural formulation of the counter-culture—is going to be different in substance and in political enactment from the former critique of the Enlightenment by romanticism.

The great legal historian Maitland once observed that justice is secreted in the interstices of procedure. Similarly, concealed in the current struggles within university education is the conflict between the prevailing values of cognitive rationality and the expressive values of new visions of richer ways of life. Whether the visions are called "educational reform" or "restructuring the university," in the politics of education the issues between the old established culture in the universities and the new counter-culture on the periphery are being joined.

Politics is the medium for the embodiment of cultural imaginations in social structures. Stories and their characters created by the imagination must be submitted to the disciplines of politics if they are to be enacted in the social world. It is of some importance, therefore, to inquire into the political resources of those committed to policies of cognitive rationality and of those committed to the visions of the counter-culture. The context of this query is unstable, complex, and surprising. When inquiry is made into the resources for political action of these ways of life one finds wide divergences, as is to be expected. What is surprising, however, is that unexpected convergences also appear.

The dominant culture and its counter-players share an impressive set of common assumptions, perhaps more than either group prefers to admit. This is not to say, of course, that holding certain outlooks in common means that the political translations of these values in negotiation and practice will be the same. The oppositional postures become sharper when they are expressed in political action. It is possible, of course, that the political practice of both parties is better than their theories.

Since politics occurs in particular localities, it is not possible to describe here the difference in political practice. It is necessary to examine both the dominant academic culture's outlook and the sensibilities and imaginations of the dissenting counter-cultures.

There is a cluster of terms having a common field of meaning: *process, interaction, participation.* In sociology, systems theory, the sciences, art, and psychology, these words are worn smooth by much use. They seem to represent for their users, professional and lay, important ways of understanding phenomena. In their use they display important elements that are shared by established and dissenting groups. As Kenneth Keniston says:

In emphasizing "style" rather than ideology, program, or characteristics, I mean to suggest that the communalities in postmodern youth groups are to be found in the way *they approach the world, rather than in their actual behavior, ideologies, or goals. Indeed, the focus on process rather than program is itself a prime characteristic of the postmodern style, reflecting a world where flux is more obvious than fixed purpose.*[12]

Ackerman makes a similar point:

It is not just in the natural sciences that what once were described in commonsense terms as discrete bodies or objects have come to be described in terms of interactions—that, for instance, observers of the biochemical interaction of the human organism with the environment speak of the body as a process rather than an entity. Similarly, in twentieth-century abstract painting, the representation of distinct commonsense objects located in a measurable pictorial space has given way to the invention of complex interplays of colors, line, planes, and shapes which eliminate the polarity of object and space. The scientist and the artist both are interested in relationship functions; they have been asking how the elements with which they deal behave with respect to one another rather than what they "really" are, or how they appear to be in the commonsense world. . . . The breakdown of the barriers between observer and the thing

[12] K. Keniston, "Youth, Change and Violence," *American Scholar,* 1968, *37*(2), 228.

observed (in the modern physics and the study of perception) has affected the arts themselves, as when the audience enters the arena of the actor in the theater, or, as more recently, in only partially planned "happenings," in which the viewer participates; or when sculpture becomes "environmental," sharing and invading the locus of everyday action; or, again, when the composer of a musical composition instructs the performer to select the order in which its passages are to be performed.[13]

It is not hard to find additional examples of the permeation of the culture at large by the idioms of interaction, process, and participation. The sense of discreteness of acts or bodies; the sense of collapse between object and space; the sense that any arrest of interacting processes, for example, in making a statement about processes, is an impossible deformation; the sense that the enduring self is updated in celebrations of consciousness which are indeterminate, flexible, and dynamic; the sense that space must be reduced to intimacy, instead of being a place for action; and the sense that time is not temporal sequences but is contained in the radical present, the atemporal "moment" are aspects of the emerging sensibility which are difficult to attach to any one cultural group or any one expression of the contemporary imagination. As Robert Coles comments:

I hear people say to me now—including some of the existential analysts—we haven't got time, time for long analyses—we must confront one another at the moment, immediately, in an overwhelming way. And I find myself feeling old-fashioned, and saying, but we have *to have time—time to get to know one another, slowly, tentatively, suspiciously, gratefully, surely, confidently. It* takes *time. It takes time for these things to happen: time is distance, time is the gentleness of coming to understand another person; and how can we do anything else but "take" it, time? But yet we live in an age where apparently time itself has gone through a transformation. The time that it took Lindbergh to cross the ocean, those long hours, the thirty-three and a third hours are now becoming minutes.*

[13] Ackerman, *loc. cit.*, pp. 17ff.

The analytic hours are becoming briefer and briefer, and the time itself is becoming short, perhaps fatally so. Wars can take a moment, and the world can be destroyed. And what do we get in art? We get passages like Selby's; we get Brillo ads on canvas. And I feel myself getting old and tired, reactionary, and on the defensive. And yet maybe we can connect all this through that word ritualization; *and wonder whether there isn't a breakdown affecting the artist, the writer, the warrior, the political leader, the psychiatrist, anyone, affecting the educator with his computer, which he's told he must use, and affecting some essential aspects of humanity, having to do with words and experiences like* distance, *and* respect, *and* sensibility, *and a sense of carefulness. And the word* craft, *which means* time *and thought and leisure—whether that, too, isn't so fatally collapsing that there is a breakdown in what you could call ritualization.*[14]

Possibly the counter-cultures of dissent and new vision are best understood as the radicalizing of values, techniques, and sensibilities both manifest and latent in modern culture in general and in some important aspects of the reigning academic culture in particular.

One of the major expressions of the new sensibility is in music. But this music requires for its production major and sophisticated technological support. What does this technology, and perhaps other technologies as well, have in common with the musical experience?

Technology, the ground on which the two realms of history and nature have met and interpenetrated each other in our time, points back to the connection between the concept of nature and history. . . . The connection lies in the concept of process: both imply that we think and consider everything in terms of process and are not concerned with single entities or individual occurrences and their special separate causes. . . . What the concept of process implies is that the concrete and the general, the single thing or event and

[14] R. Coles, *The American Scholar,* symposium on "Violence in Literature," 1968, *37*(3), 491–492.

the universal meaning, have parted company. The process, which alone makes meaningful whatever it happens to carry along, has thus acquired a monopoly of universality and significance.[15]

Seen in this light, the technology and the experience it makes possible, for example, in modern music, are not enemies but collaborators in the nurturing of modern sensibility. Nothing is more central to the counter-culture than musical forms that men of the Enlightenment find odd, to say the least, yet nothing is more indicative of the triumph of the Enlightenment than technology which, in its electronic manifestations, is so central to the production of modern music. However, many expressions of the counter-culture's music must be read as radical rejections of the machine culture which makes both technology and music possible. This collaboration, long in the making and deep in modern cultural movements, represents an outlook on the world that can best be described as esthetic. Sontag speaks of "the debilitating effects of our habit of over-estheticizing revolution." She also remarks that "American radicals have not yet learned what is functional much less essential to their revolution, and to the society they aspire to build. All they know is that such a society must be built, and both its means and its end is a new kind of consciousness. They know, too, that that consciousness involves a higher kind of moral aspiration, but the strongest form into which they can put their moral insights so far is more esthetic than political."[16]

The primary category of modern esthetics is immediacy. And music is the best medium of immediacy. "Music always expresses the immediate in its immediacy. . . ."[17] The concepts of

[15] H. Arendt, "The Concept of History: Ancient and Modern," in *Between Past and Future* (New York: Viking, 1961), pp. 61, 64. See also J. H. Miller, *Poets of Reality* (Cambridge: The Belknap Press, 1966), p. 4, on the complementary aspects of modern technology and romanticism: "The devouring nothingness of consciousness is the will to power over things. The will wants to assimilate everything to itself, to make everything a reflection within its mirror. Seen from this perspective, romanticism and technology appear to be similar rather than antithetical."

[16] S. Sontag, "Some Thoughts on the Right Way (for us) to Love the Cuban Revolution," *Ramparts*, 1969, 7(11), 18, 19.

[17] S. Kierkegaard, *Either/Or*, Vol. I, ed. Howard Johnson (Garden City, N.Y.: Anchor, 1969), p. 68.

participation, interaction, and process, when appropriated by the radicalizing culture, become essentially ways of expressing experience in esthetic modes. The crucial issue is whether it is possible to move on the basis of an esthetic culture of vision and immediate experience to a world of moral action and political practice. In the background, significant for an understanding of the cultural warfare of the present, are two traditions which, while having major oppositional values, cultivate similar outlooks; it is important to notice that both these traditions have their spokesmen and their media for expression in the modern university as well as on its periphery. Each tradition has affiliations with both the Enlightenment and romanticism.

The first tradition may be called scientism, radical empiricism, or various brands of positivism. This outlook denies the value of tradition, perhaps because the Enlightenment itself was in revolt against inherited prejudices and superstitions. This explains why the latter-day successors of the *philosophes* fail to appreciate any historical pattern that is not seen as progressive and why they reject the past as a category for understanding human discontents. Advocates and practitioners of this tradition are committed to testing everything received; they are committed to skepticism. Kant's "age of criticism" has continued.

It is the tradition which demands the avoidance of every extraneous impediment to the precise perception of reality, regardless of whether that impediment comes from tradition, from institutional authority, or internal passion or impulse. It is critical of the arbitrary and the irrational. In its emphasis on the indispensability of firsthand and direct experience, it sets itself in opposition to everything which comes between the mind of the knowing individual and "reality." It is easy to see how social convention and the traditional authority associated with institutions would fall prey to the ravages of this powerfully persuasive and corrosive tradition.[18]

It is not difficult to see in this description attitudes which

[18] E. Shils, "The Intellectuals and the Powers: Some Perspectives for Comparative Analysis," *Comparative Studies in Society and History,* 1958, *1*(1), 18–19.

are both similar to and different from the romantic tradition. It is also easy to understand why those academic persons who inherit and perpetuate this outlook are ill-prepared to appreciate the politics of the university as an institution. Akin to this outlook is what Philip Rieff has called the "analytic attitude,"[19] a radical commitment to what Polanyi calls "unbridled lucidity."[20]

This is the educated capacity for entertaining multiple perspectives on oneself, one's data, one's premises, one's world. Scepticism of oneself, data, and rules is part of the process. Not only does this sensibility use ambiguity and scepticism as tools, these tools inform a way of relating to the world by way of distance and doubt. What doubt is to reason, despair is to the person. The world not only becomes elusive and problematic, so does the self which relates to such a world. A sense of unreality in relation to world and self results. In the search for immediate testing of reality, there is a paradoxical loss of connection with reality.

Two processes are generated by this view of knowing. On the one hand, the knowing self systematically retreats before the analysis of its actions into what Gilbert Ryle has called the "systematic elusiveness of I"[21] until there is no legitimate way to account for its integrity. On the other hand, the world of nature becomes ultimately a field of mathematically controlled forces. The universe is reduced to a contentless consciousness and to an encompassing field of interacting processes. (I suggest that the celebrations of consciousness, so much alluded to in the literature of the new culture, bear an undetected kinship with this view of knowledge sponsored by the very academy which the advocates of the new culture are attacking.) The practitioners of the analytic attitude need confirmation of the self and of the world, since both have been dissolved by explorations into regions of inner experience about which nothing can be said and from which nothing can be intended, much less performed, in the public world of time and space.

In this connection Freud's thought and his influence on so-

[19] P. Rieff, "Analytic Attitude," *Encounter Magazine,* 1954, *18*(6), 22.

[20] Polanyi, *op. cit.,* Chapter One.

[21] G. Ryle, *The Concept of Mind* (New York: Barnes and Noble, 1949), pp. 195–198.

ciety offer a fascinating example of the convergence and divergence of cultural confusions. Freud was a man of the Enlightenment—where the id was, there shall the ego be. This is the program of the rational attitude in relation to the self. Yet he also knew about an older wisdom—the truth about human selves is to be discovered in a forgotten fateful encounter in *Ur*-history, in the dark world of pre-history, in myth. Despite Freud's tragic sense of life, the Enlightenment program triumphs in the end, for his therapeutic program is dedicated to rational control. But this control is to be sought in the privacy of therapy because *Ur*-history is not the arena of political, that is, human, action. Persons do not meet one another politically in their dreams. Consequently, the private time and space of the therapeutic hour become the *polis*. The problem of how to connect personal history with communal history or personal selves with public institutions still remains. This question both bridges and separates the conflict between the older culture of the Enlightenment and the newer cultures of spontaneity. For both cultures the status of action in the political realm is problematic.

If radical reflection generates ambiguity about word and intention, and their possible connections, action has unchallengeable authenticity. Action is unmediated sincerity, a quality, or a virtue, always to be doubted when the medium is words or stories. The greater the doubt or ambiguity, or the less intentional the dispositions of consciousness, the more intense is the need for inviolate expressions of sincerity and for confirming engagements with the world outside the self. In this view, violence—in imagination or in action—may appear as the most honest act of confirmation: both actor and acted upon are confirmed in their togetherness and distance; and ambiguity of intentions is overcome in merciful suspensions of doubt.

The romantic tradition, born in part as a negative response to the Enlightenment tradition, mounts its opposition to the impersonal world of scientism with radical affirmations of spontaneity, of originality, of novelty. This view considers the life of reason self-destructive, especially in the detached, "cool" perspective of the man of reason. Impulse and inconsistency are not viewed as defections, and the ecstatic often becomes of primary importance.

However, this tradition shares important features with Enlightenment rationalism, its presumed enemy. Both traditions suspect any mediation between the self and the world. For example, both outlooks share a fundamentally negative evaluation of institutions. "Institutions which have rules and which prescribe the conduct of the individual members by conventions and commands are likewise viewed as life-destroying."[22]

While one tradition accentuates reflective immediacy, the other emphasizes sensuous immediacy. These traditions do not occur with separateness and distinctness in contemporary culture. They have undergone multiple transformations which do not respect the classifications of difference and similarity noted here. The advocates and practitioners of sensuous immediacy, who arrange counter-festivals to the predominant system and sensibility of Enlightenment values, assume that they are attacking a system repugnant to their "new" culture, and indeed they are. What few of these representatives realize is that their grounds for attack, in many ways, are dependent on the enemy. What is taken for liberation turns out to be only another form of bondage to the dominant traditions.

The advocates and practitioners of reflective immediacy, or the rational attitude, are usually not aware of their contributions to those movements they perceive as their radical critics. It is not difficult to understand why both traditions, in their confusions, are not able to endorse a view of things which provides for public space, action, and history—all of which categories are central to political reflection and political action.

On rather primitive epistemological grounds it is possible to appreciate why each of these traditions has an attitude of suspicion toward procedures, committees, due process, and roles, and why they no longer believe there is representation within the university. All these manners, customs, and beliefs are perceived as devices which produce distance between persons; they displace immediacy. In the tradition of spontaneity, with its distrust of words as mere rhetoric,[23] it is possible for violence to be embraced as a way of

[22] Shils, *loc. cit.*, p. 19.

[23] See G. Steiner, "The Retreat from the Word," *Kenyon Review*, 1961, *23*(2), 187–216.

overcoming distance; violence is seen not as act, but as experience, as participation in a creative process. Such violence is the rejection of politics; it is esthetic experience.

The reason the present situation is so pregnant with both creative and destructive possibilities is that, against the background of these two traditions, there is increasing intensity of moral passion. In the complex convergence and divergence of intellectual traditions the present generation has found a powerful moral passion that the intellectual traditions they have inherited ill equip them to articulate and manage.

The rationalists, with their commitment to cognitive rationality, have no way of affirming with confidence their moral beliefs, including the belief in cognitive rationality, because the person as moral actor has disappeared in their theory. Moral convictions do not meet the tests of the analytic attitude. Moral beliefs like justice are intangible, they find no place in a theory of knowledge which celebrates only critical intelligence. Critical intelligence is not guided by norms of how and when to use it. Embarrassed in the presence of moral conviction, especially their own, the rationalists keep moral commitments separate or smuggle them through various techniques of "pseudo-substitution."[24]

The new cultures of dissent and counter-vision are vital with moral passion, but they consider that any norm (which partakes of some measure of universality and, therefore, is available to many different groups) is static, a freezing of what is inherently dynamic, personal, and open. Yet there is no such thing as an open morality —there is only a set of moral beliefs, which must be more than the intensity of an individual's sincerity, which endorses empathy and tolerance, and which must therefore have regard for both self and others. Only a set of moral beliefs grounded in some order beyond (yet including) the existential order of the person can support an ethic of openness and a politics of mutuality. To connect moral acts by identifying them as moral, an order different from the immediate experience of moral acts must be acknowledged. Yet, such

[24] See M. Polanyi, *Personal Knowledge: Towards a Post-Critical Philosophy* (London: Routledge and Kegan Paul, 1958), pp. 16, 147, 166, 169–70, 371–372. Polanyi has articulated a theory of knowledge that endorses and gives theoretical support for moral beliefs.

considerations appear to many of the new culture as abstract and mediate, hence unreal. Moral passion is not the same as moral action; and moral passion to remain moral must have access to means of criticism and correction. Without such criteria and without some procedures for criticism and correction, communities founded on moral passion may be tragically transformed into communities of quite other descriptions.

If moral passion remains at the level of personal immediacy because the culture offers no subsidy for its containment, there is no possibility for moral reflection, retrospective or prospective. Yet if the only theory of knowledge available to the morally passionate cannot account for its own commitment to the goodness of knowing, much less account for the intangible character of other moral norms, it is understandable that moral passion frequently flirts with nihilism.

I suggest that it is the intermingling and confusions of the university's own intellectual traditions that need exploration before new stories for future action can be told. Instead of confessing the sins of the larger society, which, of course, shares in many of these same traditions, men and women who work in universities need to attend to their own. Perhaps a period of fasting should precede the decision to join any festivals, new or old, dominant or counter.

Edward Joseph Shoben, Jr.

University and Society

III

All of us live in an ambiguous but irresistibly determining world of time. We are conditioned by our past, both collectively and in the most personal ways. We are responsive to an always intrusive and compelling present, that now in which our needs and desires are most strongly felt; and we cannot avoid the anticipation of some future, immediate or remote, in which our disappointment silently waits for us. There is a sense in which much of what we mean by liberation, presumably one of the major goals of a liberal education, is some significant transcendence of our past conditionings and of our present parochialisms of need and experience. The mechanism of transcendence is that of functionally understanding oneself and of discovering those options which the wider world presents and which, when worked on by the cultivated imagination, provide a man of self-knowledge with the stuff out of which he can in some meaningful fashion shape and invent his future rather than be captured by it.

Various institutions serve, well or badly, to establish the conditions for liberation. The task is difficult for a variety of reasons, not the least of which is the staggering diversity of human traits and human aspirations that must be taken into account. The university should be judged largely as such an institution. In its educational undertaking (and it has others), its proper business is the personal development of its members, particularly its students, as the processes of personal development bear on the dynamics of liberation. When it attends creatively and vigorously to this central business, the university is a major agent of social change despite its inherent political incapacities and despite the fact that it can do little through direct intervention to affect the quality of present society and culture.

Whatever the character of its internal relations, the university in our time is not an isolate, effectively insulated from the larger society. Its transactions with the world, whether it executes them well or badly, are both inevitable and complex; and because those transactions are by no means entirely independent of one another, the effectiveness with which it manages one may determine in important ways its success in coping with another. Ultimately, many of its central internal qualities as a place of education may be functions of the style and the conceptual clarity with which it interacts with its surroundings—its surroundings defined both by geography and by that network of relationships in which it is enmeshed and to which it must be responsive.

For example, the university is both in and of a neighborhood. In consequence, the ethic of neighborliness obtains. The university owes its neighbors a full measure of respect for their rights and interests, and when its special concerns conflict, as they may, with theirs, it must scrupulously observe the rules of negotiation that apply among neighbors. Its resources should be subject to mobilization to serve their needs in appropriate ways, and the university and its neighbors should be ready to form such alliances as may be called for to solve common problems that beset the neighborhood. Such obvious propositions reflect less the pieties of abstract morality than the realities of experience. A university must live in reasonable harmony with its neighbors to enjoy its own self-realization, and the health and security of its neighborhood are likely to affect significantly its own health and security. Clearly, there is every reason for reciprocity in these interchanges; but because the university as neighbor is likely either to be big and powerful or to appear big and powerful (and the distinction is only rarely of practical consequence), the university is under the obligation to make its case with all possible gentleness when it needs the respect, the services, and the alliances that it is ready to accord to others.

But if the university is a neighbor in the local sense, it is also, in the wider society, an institution that serves a particular set of functions. It is in its institutional role that it carries on its regional, national, and international transactions, and it is for serving that particular set of functions that the larger society supports it. Those institutionalized and socially supported functions are, in general, the expanding of man's cognitive horizons through scholarship and critical thought and the educating of students through the facilitation of learning, including formal teaching.

As neighbor and as institution, the university is subject to role conflicts. The ancient tension between town and gown is probably inherent and only more massive and more complicated in its contemporary forms than in earlier forms. A university cannot dismiss its students for their occasional boisterousness on the streets or their tendency to mob the local coffee houses or overflow the beer parlors. In a state built economically on milk and butter, it cannot fire the nutritionist whose research reveals the virtues of margarine. When the John Birch Society or some comparable group attacks Castro sympathizers, the university must protect its Cuban mathematician and its Marxist historian of revolutions. If there are local objections to classroom discussions of sex, it cannot expunge Lawrence and Burroughs from recent literary history or pretend that Kinsey never issued his bulky reports. Should the district attorney and police chief condemn its students for their alleged use of marijuana, the university cannot ignore the differences between cannabis and heroin, between an intoxicant and a narcotic, or accept the peculiar logic that contends that because most drug addicts have smoked pot, all pot-smokers will become drug addicts.

But neither, as a good neighbor, can a university flaunt its institutional characteristics or claim exemptions from the law to which all others are subject. Sanctuary, if it was ever an academic prerogative, has been part of the price of secularization; and the bravura mode of insisting on public acceptance of the views for which the university provides a home contravenes the conditions of neighborliness, ignores what is known of the social psychology of persuasion, and implies an assumption of authority and insight that flirts more with arrogance than with accuracy.

At the same time, there is a fuzzy but strong entailment in our observations so far: when the neighborly and the institutional are at variance within the university, the institutional commitments must prevail. To test this proposition and to clarify the issues bound up with it, it may be helpful to examine the often reviewed but never settled questions of what kind of institution a university is, and what its basic functions are that provide it with its necessary support and give it leverage in its transactions with the larger society.

It is currently fashionable to search for models in our efforts to comprehend more fully the university as an institution. Thus, the university is studied as a corporation, as a quasi-governmental department, as a training school operated by a particular social class, and so on. All these angles are useful, and each validly reveals some important aspect of a university's operations that might otherwise be overlooked. But there is a peculiarity in the approach through credible models. When we attempt to understand other institutions—the family, for instance—we are less likely to conceptualize them by their approximations to models than we are to ask how they may be conceived in and of themselves. At the very least, it is as legitimate to search for the distinctive and differentiating characteristics that define the university as it is to identify its similarities to a business firm, a governmental agency, a training school, or whatever.

Considered in itself, the university—regardless of what else it may be—emerges as a place where any issue of human significance can be considered intellectually without limitation. If universities have often failed to realize themselves fully on this score, the failures rest more on the imperfections of the mortal men who operate them than on the inappropriateness of the conception. Actually, this defining notion is a very old one, almost as old as the Western universities themselves. For example, the social organization of medieval institutions provided an opportunity within the curriculum for controversial social problems to be examined by faculty and students. Within this framework, Stephen Langton, lecturing at Paris in the twelfth century, worked out the "theoretical justification for the opposing of tyrants" on the basis of which he later, as archbishop of Canterbury, confronted King John. Indeed, much of the history of academic freedom (in the sense of *Lehrfreiheit*) revolves around the establishment and defense of just this principle of unfettered intellectual exploration as the definiendum of the university. If the battle for liberty in inquiry, in study, and in the evaluation of ideas is almost surely a never ending one, an index of its victories to date is reassuringly available in the Supreme Court's Keyishian decision of 1966. There, for the first time, academic freedom, characterized as "of transcendent value to all of us and not merely to the teachers concerned," is regarded as "a special concern" of the First Amendment.

Nevertheless, academic freedom has inevitably had its price, paid in the form of "institutional neutrality." The meaning of this term, however, is slippery, and its clarification resides more in shifting collegial and public policies than it does in any hard and fast definition. In general, it implies that an institution centered on intellectual exploration and criticism differs from a political institution in the ways in which it is related to society at large. For example, it has no official political ideology. Similarly, it attempts neither to elect candidates nor to effect by advocacy or by campaigning the passage of particular laws, except when there is a clear and present danger to the university itself. The rise of Nazi power in the 1930s and early 1940s and the demagoguery of McCarthy in the 1950s are cases in point. In other instances, the neighbor status of a particular university may require involvement in the political process in some fashion.

But there are difficulties here. The first lies in the question of who speaks for a university: When and under what circumstances does the institution, rather than some component part of it, find a voice? If a faculty adopts, unanimously or by a split vote, a resolution against the war in Vietnam, does it speak for the university? If the president expresses himself as favoring a federal civil rights bill, does he represent an institutional view? If students demonstrate outside the House Office Building against the existence of the House Un-American Activities Committee, is theirs a political act on behalf of the university in which they are registered? The answer is negative in all cases. The institution speaks through only those persons who have the authority to implement the statements made. Thus, the voice of the university is clear when its purchasing agent signs an order for office furniture or a computer, when an appropriate faculty body decides a curricular issue, or when a duly empowered officer signs a contract for the construction of a new laboratory. Politically, then, universities are institutionally neutral because they are organized in such a fashion that they can only with special effort express themselves in a univocal manner. That lack of univocality reflects an organization that maximizes individual voices and therefore furthers the free play of ideas in the intellectual marketplace. It also provides much of the basis on which the institution can claim protection for particular members of its official personnel. Because its business is with the examination and criticism of ideas, and not with their direct translation into law or public policy, it can throw a mantle of safety around professors (or, with increasing frequency, students) who step to a different intellectual drummer. The Genovese case at Rutgers is only one of many examples of this.

But this difficulty leads to two related ones. First, the gap between principle and practice is always a bit troublesome even when it is narrow. In the domain of academic freedom, with its entailment of institutional neutrality, the gap can be large. Unpopular ideas and unconventional conduct, when they emanate from a campus, are typically perceived either as reflecting an institutional position or as somehow constituting evidence that the university is unsupportive of the society which finances it and of which it is a part. Such perceptions define a segment of the social reality with which universities must deal, and it is rarely easy to maintain a principle pure and undefiled in a day-to-day context filled with the impurities and defilements that arise because men are not angels and operating societies are not utopias. Second, if the university's central task is the intellectual examination of any issue that is looked upon as humanly significant, that task is complicated by two factors not often seriously considered: Ideas have consequences; and because it can be argued that ideas are not fully understood unless those consequences have been appropriately tested, it is quite possible that meaningful intellectual exploration may require experience beyond the boundaries of a campus, or experience which demands changes in the internal qualities of campus life. This proposition, when it is related to the educational mission of the university as a place for intellectual exploration, raises sharp questions about the goals of education, the nature of learning and teaching, and the ways in which institutions and society must interact to facilitate learning and teaching and to permit the achievement of those goals. Each of these broad problems—the one having to do with the implications of how a university is perceived, the other centering on the character of its educational responsibilities—must be pressed a little further.

With respect to its public image, the university is caught in another of its several inherent tensions. Whatever its cultural context (Moscow, Oxford, New York, or Peking), higher education is institutionally maintained to enhance and to give continuity to the society in which it is inevitably embedded. At the same time, it is a device for cultivating the brainpower and encouraging the creative resources that, at different rates in different periods and patterns of life, ultimately modify that society. Simultaneously, then, universities are conservative agencies and forces for social change. In the United States, the balance has never been easy; it has varied at any given time from institution to institution, and it has been determined essentially (which is not a synonym for wholly) by the larger community's shifting consensus about its most urgent needs.

The point about the balance between conservative and change-oriented impulses is a crucial one. American universities have from the first been responsive to national opinion; their strong vocational slant, especially toward professional preparation and (during the past hundred years) the development of technically trained manpower, is a reflection of that responsiveness. Harvard's seventeenth-century emphasis on the production of Christian ministers for the wilderness of the New World, the early and rapid absorption of medical schools into universities, the establishment of the land-grant colleges for the furtherance of "agriculture and the mechanic arts," the charging of universities with the task of fitting budding lawyers for the bar examinations, the investment of the universities in massive research and special training activities during the two world wars, and the burgeoning of academically based science after the ascent of Sputnik are only a few of the historic indicators of this intimate involvement of higher education with society. If that involvement has put a premium on the growth of business and industry, on service to government, and on opportunities for the socially advantaged and the economically ambitious, it has been because clear national sentiment and well-supported policy favored such a harnessing of America's intellectual resources to the building of a strong middle class and to the expansionist dynamics of its commercial enterprises. At the same time, the universities were consistently under fire at one place or another for their tolerance and their very encouragement of criticism from within their faculties of the same public interests that they served.

A great deal of the ambivalence in the United States toward higher education stems from these opposing tendencies within our institutions; and if universities are perceived as strange amalgams of staunch pillars of the American way and hotbeds of radicalism, it is because they have maintained a degree of capaciousness for both conservative and critical functions, for responding to the officially formulated needs of the country, and for subjecting those needs to sharp and not always friendly examination. But this kind of intellectual capaciousness has also meant, and currently means, that colleges are constantly in a defensive position by virtue of the confused image they project. On the one hand, they draw fire from political and social conservatives because of their insistence on protecting independent and dissenting thought and its expression; on the other, they are under duress from liberal and radical factions for their service to the establishment. And they repeatedly must make clear the necessity for increasing financial support from legislatures and private donors in spite of ambiguity as to how that support will affect the conservative-critical balance in their many-faceted operations.

At the moment, that ambiguity is exceptionally high, inside the university as well as without. A comparison here of the zeitgeist of 1942 with that of 1970 may be instructive. At the time of Pearl Harbor, in spite of strong previous currents of antiwar feeling, national policy and national sentiment were unified. If the war against Hitler's Germany and Hirohito's Japan was a matter of both terror and sadness, it was regarded as morally necessary and represented a cause for which the overwhelming majority of decent men were quite willing to take risks. The contrast with the war in Vietnam is shocking. Great numbers of us, not pacifists by background or persuasion, look upon it as a gross immorality and are shamed by our country's prosecution of it. There is no cause involved that commands our willingness to bear risks; and for a great many of us, the interests of decency run exactly counter to the interests served by America's involvement in Southeast Asia. The contrast in public sentiment reflects itself in the universities. In World War II, there was no meaningful objection to the various military training programs undertaken by the academy, the heavy involvement of universities in war-related research, and the accommodation of the resources of higher education to the recognized needs for industrial and military manpower. On the contrary, such activities were almost universally applauded. In contrast, a large share of the most articulate criticism of the war in Vietnam has stemmed from our institutions of higher learning; faculty members have aided students in resisting the draft as a mechanism for abetting the war, and academic suspicion runs high with respect to many of the connections between university-based research and its application by the military. At the same time, there are still those within the university who, because of their own different convictions, give assent to the war and put their talents at its service.

Around this complicated state of affairs revolves a set of profoundly important issues that bear on the moral climate of the university and the tacit ethical commitments that its institutional distinctiveness requires. A part of the public charge to the academy is the discovery of new knowledge, the creative resynthesis of knowledge, and the critical evaluation of knowledge—the functions that define research. The research mandate is an essential one for three basic reasons. First, the society of which the university is integrally and inescapably a part feeds on the products of inquiry, sometimes with enthusiasm and sometimes with reluctance but always out of a central necessity of our age. Second, institutions of higher learning carry, by definition, a prime responsibility for rolling back the frontiers of human ignorance, for extending public comprehension of the world and its history, including man himself and his varieties of culture. Finally, without the exercise of discovery, resynthesis, and critical evaluation, universities cannot render adequate educational services. Unless they are deeply concerned with the active enlarging of men's understanding, they can offer only static or doctrinaire educational experiences that are of little use or relevance in our rapidly changing society.

Human understanding, however, is never complete, never final. Discovery, resynthesis, and critical evaluation exist in uneasy and often dissident relationships with one another, and a university is a place in which comprehension is advanced through continuous, sophisticated, and informed debate. As open-minded participants in that debate, the citizens of a university have an opportunity to change their minds and to grow by casting off earlier convictions that cannot stand the test of evidence and logic. In this opportunity for growth lies the necessity for intellectual freedom. For the debate to be most facilitative, it must be untrammeled except by the constraints of information, the canons of effective thought, and the limits of the imagination. Anything that puts this kind of freedom at hazard also risks the very essence of a liberating education.

Nevertheless, knowledge and the ideas that organize it—the

central bases of understanding—are two-edged swords. The myth of Eden is not the only ancient reminder that knowledge and thought can be used for ill as well as for good. The remote outcomes of research are by no means entirely foreseeable, and it is hard to identify a significant discovery, resynthesis, or new evaluation in the history of man whose consequences have not been, from some important vantage point, mixed. Yet the one thing that has been morally clear has been the evil in efforts to stifle or to warp the human quest for greater comprehension, for relief from ignorance.

The ethic of research, then, lies in the freedom of its pursuit of truth, in its contribution to human growth through education, and in its open and public nature. It does not lie in the unpredictable uses to which knowledge or ideas can be put, and it cannot be restricted by the political or ideological passions of a particular day or a particular group. When very different moral and social convictions, firmly and sincerely held by their proponents, are at war with one another, then conflicts about research can be wisely settled only by an appeal to the indigenous ethic of scholarship.

That ethic is tested by the difficult problems arising from the sheer expense of present research in many fields, especially but far from exclusively in the natural sciences and engineering. The federal government has become virtually the only source of support adequate to fund these costly investigations; and under the present policies and practices of the United States Congress, a very high proportion of the money for research is allocated to the Department of Defense. Because many members of the academy are wary of the role and strength of the military in our national life, and because even more are vehemently opposed to the disgraceful and brutal war in Southeast Asia, great numbers of professors and administrators are more than usually sensitive to the old dictum that how he who pays the piper calls the tune. To what extent do research contracts with the Department of Defense imply service to goals that are morally antipathetic to the university?

It seems probable that the proper answer to this crucial question lies in the closeness with which the academic community binds itself to the ethic of responsible research and in the clarity with which it rules itself by the values of intellectual freedom, human growth through education, and the public nature of inquiry. Although the source of funding is never irrelevant, neither is it a sufficient basis for judging the intellectual suitability and moral appropriateness of an investigative task. That judgment must be made by the individual scholar within the framework of institutional policies that reflect the internal morality of research; and that judgment must always be made in an atmosphere that is free from both considerations of momentary popularity and threats of personal harm, disruption, or reprisals. Recognizing that the knowledge that men discover or create can be employed destructively as well as constructively, and in order to cope with this fact without restricting the free play of intellectual freedom, institutions of higher learning need explicit regulations to govern their scholarly activity.

Those regulations should cover four major considerations. First, when an individual faculty member associates himself with a research problem, he must do so only voluntarily and not as an agent of any organization outside the university. Among other things, this condition implies that he must control the formulation of the project, the methods selected for pursuing the inquiry, and the ways in which inferences are drawn from the findings. Second, all scholarly endeavor in a university must be consonant with its educational goals and be of a kind that permits students to participate in a meaningful fashion. Third, in all instances of sponsored research, the principal investigator must have final authority over who is employed on his project, and employment must be based solely on evidence of academic and professional competence, unencumbered by considerations of race, ethnic background, religious belief, or political persuasion. And finally, all the results and conclusions of any study must be publishable in the open literature and thus made directly available to the technical scrutiny of other scholars and to the moral evaluation of the public. These reports should not be subject to any kind of prepublication review by the sponsoring agency, and the agency may exercise no control over public reflections on the implications and significance of the work by any member of the research staff.

Under such regulations, classified research would obviously

be inadmissible on the campus as a violation of the principles of intellectual freedom, human growth through education, and the public nature of academic inquiry. Should any sponsoring body require classification of a project in progress, the contract would have to be canceled. In the case of the Department of Defense, it is noteworthy that, over a period of more than twenty years, it has funded research under conditions described by the general policies suggested here. Although its standard contract permits the Department of Defense to recommend the classification at any time of originally unclassified projects, there is no evidence that it has exercised that contractual right from 1950 to 1970. In any event, demands for classification must, under the guidelines derived from the ethic of academic investigation, be met by prompt cancellation.

Given these regulations, a university must still recognize that such issues as the relationship of intellectual effort in the modern age to the national security and to American military development are deeply debatable. Men of goodwill and incontestable principle can differ passionately along many moral lines. For some, the reasons for bitterly opposing United States intervention in Vietnam are precisely the same as those for just as bitterly regretting the failure of the United States to intervene in Spain in 1936 and for being proud, in spite of the nightmares that recur after so many years, that they were involved in World War II. Argument about such matters must be encouraged, and ways must be found to infuse those arguments with a richer stock of information and of setting them in a context of ever widening understanding of the complex problems that are entailed. Each faculty member and each student, however, must enjoy the right to follow the dictates of his own conscience in making decisions about his scholarly investments, just as no one may be allowed to interfere with the enjoyment of that same right by others. No university can be great, significant, or even adequate if its members must cling to a single, monolithic political or moral norm.

At the same time, there is no denying that the American academy has moved, since World War II, into an increasing dependence on the mushrooming affairs of the state. Rooted in the larger society, it has become progressively more responsive to national manpower requirements, to needs for applied knowledge to fuel the engines of industry, government, and the military, and to pleas (sweetened by dollars) for relatively short-range aid in relieving urban and other social pressures. Simultaneously, however, its resources as a repository of humanistic learning and thought have increased; and despite the urgency of continuing protective vigilance, the university remains a place where critical intellectual analysis and the friendly examination of values that run counter to those of the corporation and of government's officialdom can proceed in an essentially untrammeled way. Much of the condemnation of the war in Vietnam has emanated from an academic core, and dissident students have found nowhere else the free forum for their ideas that their colleges have quite explicitly furnished.

Once again, then, we witness a clash—larger in scope and more intense than, but in direct lineage from, historical precedents —between the humane and deliberately critical outlook of the university and its obligations as what Clark Kerr called a knowledge factory. If it produces the technicians and the technical expertise demanded by an increasingly technical and highly organized society, it also sponsors opposition to technological trends and underwrites the quest for alternatives to them. In a framework of rapid communication and breakaway social change, this sort of tension often becomes deeply stressful and difficult to manage in a fashion that is either intellectually or developmentally constructive.

Yet it is into the context of this articulate tension that the university takes huge numbers of young people from their families and their neighborhoods without their having yet established their own connections through marriage, careers, or property. Fraternities, social clubs, or the process of working one's way through college once tied students more firmly to the traditions of family or the norms of social class; the conditions of postindustrial society make these devices either too elitist to play a significant part in an atmosphere of mass education or insufficiently necessary under programs of government scholarships and low-interest loans. As a consequence, student bodies comprise, to an important degree, people whom Kenneth Keniston identifies as "psychological adults but sociological adolescents," that is, persons who lack "the prime sociological characteristic of adulthood: integration into the institutional structures of society."[1]

The interaction between these two traits of the contemporary academy—the strain between service to and criticism of official society, and the significant presence of sociological adolescents creates an environment keenly hospitable to progressive intellectual analysis and humanistic values. Because they occupy a marginal status, students are naturally drawn to ideological and normative perspectives at variance with the societal mode, and this kind of attraction is bitterly emphasized when their integration into the institutional structures is likely to be by an inequitable and suspect selective service system. For a farsighted left, such a situation is an opportunity to develop the theories, generate the analyses, and create the alternative social programs that might alter over time the character of the country's political and cultural consciousness. By introducing a new spirit and new prospects into the ongoing debates about national policy and the qualities of our social life, such an effort could in the long run shape new majorities and achieve quite genuinely radical—and humanely democratic—ends. Although protest demonstrations and third-party campaigns on particular issues (like Eugene McCarthy's) would have important values, solid accomplishments would depend on the hard, disciplined work of inventing, communicating, and applying in limited ways—quite conceivably to the processes of university governance themselves—the social forms that characterize real and viable options to the technological extrapolations forecast for us.

But the very fact that students occupy a marginal status obstructs efforts to develop this kind of intellectual and democratic radical effort in the university. As marginal men, students are disposed to cultivate a radicalism of self-conscious alienation, a symbolic politics, and a nihilistic militancy in which the nature of the gestures made and the momentary triumphs over the establishment are more gratifying than the achievement of carefully planned and relatively well-envisioned changes of a substantive sort. In today's world, this kind of romanticism is neither incomprehensible nor un-

[1] *The Uncommitted: Alienated Youth in American Society* (New York: Harcourt Brace Jovanovich, 1965).

deserving of sympathy and support; its productivity, however, is highly dubious. It is likely to retain its strength until ways are found to involve students in the formal institutions beyond the university under conditions that permit their concretizing the critical values to which so many of them are abstractly committed. Progressive thought and progressive action will probably yield a much richer social and economic harvest when they are not regarded as the distinctive property or province of youth and youth's student elite.

The conflicts within the contemporary university mirror the conflicts in the country as a whole. They are symptoms neither of higher education's disarticulation from the problems of society nor of its impotence. When honest men explore humanly significant issues without limitation, they are likely to disagree. A central part of a university's business is to develop and maintain an environment in which these disagreements can be sustained and nurtured. That environment, however, to be educative, should promote the baring of the bases of disagreement, stimulate an active searching for reasonable ways of resolving conflicts, and increase the probability that one's choice of sides in a controversy will be made on progressively more sophisticated grounds. Those more sophisticated grounds comprise attention to fact or evidence, respect for ideas, and a genuine concern for human values and the human condition in all its complexity. This notion clearly includes a grappling with what Whitehead called importance, expression, and understanding as well as with the formalities of logical analysis and the content of available bodies of knowledge.

Thus, we are brought back to the question of the university's educational responsibilities. If the primary mission of the university is the untrammeled intellectual consideration of issues of human significance, then its relationship to students obviously entails their participation in this process. But what are the goals sought, and what does this kind of participation require in order for the goals to be met? Because our institutions are quite wisely structured so as to make univocality difficult, these fundamental questions cannot be answered definitively either for one college or for all colleges at any particular time. They can, however, be widely thought about; and a legitimate objection to contemporary higher education is that they seldom are kept under any systematic, serious, and imaginative review by faculties and student bodies.

As a possible contribution to the remedying of that defect, we can try to clarify further some of the terms in our characterization of the university as a place where issues of human significance can be intellectually considered without hindrance. Although the notion of significance is a profoundly complicated one, it clearly implies two elements: One is that significance is heavily dependent on experience; what is significant for each of us is largely a function of how widely and how deeply we have engaged ourselves with the world. The other is that our criteria of significance change. What is significant to a small child is not to a grown man; what is charged with meaning for a person widely and deeply familiar with the world and its ways is irrelevant to one of narrow experience and undeveloped sensitivity. But it is experience reflected upon, experience considered in the light of the best that has been said and thought in the world, that moves a man toward the fullest realization of his humanity and is most likely to contribute to his liberation.

The intellectual explorations and the concern with ideas that are the distinctive tasks of the university are humanly and educationally important, then, because they permit broader perspectives on experience. They enable us to grow in our judgments of what is significant for ourselves both as individuals and as social men, increasing in two ways our power to deal with our experience: One is by trading on the recorded mistakes and triumphs of others in coping with the human tradition; the other is by creating out of that record, acted upon by the imagination, novel instruments of concept and commitment by which to enlarge our understanding. When ideas, interacting with experience, make this kind of contribution to personal development, they further the style of the examined life, which Socrates observed was the only one worth living. One of the features of that style is a reciprocal play between moral passion and intellectual effort. The moral ideas are disciplined by cognitive criticism and the steady test of informed thought at the same time that the emotions energize and lend color to the intellect.

As is obvious but too often ignored, when ideas and the enterprises of the intellect become disconnected from experience, which is always in some fashion a highly personal affair, they become unattractively abstract and the objects of pedantry instead of devices by which the style of the examined life may be cultivated. To make this point is to remind ourselves that ideas have consequences and that the ideas are not fully understood unless those consequences are investigated and tested. That process of investigation and testing moves one back from intellectual formulations into the realm of experience, and it suggests two points about the education of students and, for that matter, the continuing education of all members of the academy. One is that the kinds of learning that an institution facilitates are as much a matter of the experience it provides through the way it conducts its internal business and the models it presents as they are a function of the ideas it makes available through its curriculum and its classroom instruction. The other point is that although a university may be the place par excellence for the intellectual aspects of the examined life, it may not be comprehensive enough to lay in educative ways the groundwork of experience to which ideas may most profitably be tied. These two propositions need some explication.

The first point can be illustrated by the issue of civil liberty as an ethical principle. We are not discussing here a legal or juridical notion, even one of constitutional status and magnitude. Rather, our focus is on the ethos that is central to what is best in the American tradition, that general moral stance that has been formulated as the keystone of our social life and which the university, as an integral part of society, can properly be expected to encourage in its students, to expect in its faculty, and to live by in its institutional, neighborly, and internally regulatory actions. The basic idea here is simply a mutual respect for diversity and a faith that a broad (but not an infinite) range of differences among both persons and institutions, nurtured under fair and peaceful conditions, will be productive of greater interest and a greater variety of opportunity and choice for all. The ethic of civil liberties is not utopian; it does not deny the reality of evil or the innate frailties of the human spirit, and it admits the necessity of constraints, such as the constraint of law and the constraint of custom. But this ethical posture also limits the constraints. Laws are acceptable only when they reflect the public philosophy and serve the widest possible interests of the people affected by them; custom has force only when it is dynamic and subject to change as the conditions of life themselves alter. If the moral outlook here is pluralistic, it implies a pluralism that is grounded in community, in a population whose members are concerned about one another and, knowing their own shortcomings, have devised mechanisms for expressing that concern.

Obviously, our defections in practice throughout American history have been grave and sometimes vicious. Racial injustice is perhaps the ugliest and most profoundly disturbing blot on the pages of both our past and our present. Yet, in spite of even this terrible chasm between moral attainment and moral aspiration, our commitment to civil liberties has represented a widely shared belief that this concept is the only one that men have been able to invent in order to protect themselves from their own ugly imperfections. It is the only ethical device that the race has hit upon for allowing maximum freedom for human impulses, interests, and ideas to jockey with each other in reasonably peaceful competition for adherents and that both permits and encourages minority attitudes and values to persist in a quest for majority support. If, as George Eliot once observed, "justice is not without us as a fact but within us as a great yearning," then the ethic of civil liberties is the route by which that yearning may be realized and objectified without destroying it by the means through which it is sought. The likelihood of more closely approximating a just pattern of human affairs is lessened when the approach lies through naked power and riot, greater when it moves through free speech, free press, free worship, free assembly, meaningful petition, the right of privacy, due process, and the other forms—not always entirely comfortable—of social relationships that emanate from the ethic of civil liberty.

At the moment, this ethical position is under strong fire. Desperate because of the frustrations bound up with Vietnam and our singularly ominous pattern of race relations, ideologically legitimized by Marcuse's peculiar notion of repressive tolerance, and emotionally vitalized by the underdogs' victories of guerilla fighters in parts of the third world, a segment of the population of the West —especially of Western youth—would scrap the morality of civil liberties as outmoded liberal baggage, replacing it with a commitment to the tactics as well as the more humane goals of today's revolutions. At times, there seems to be no disposition even to think seriously about the replacement; the focus is simply on the destruction of the tradition and the principle along with the institutions of contemporary society. One is entitled, one is even obligated, to ask why; and if one wonders openly and honestly enough, one must be struck by the frequency with which the ethic of civil liberties has been violated by our major institutions, including our universities. These violations define a good deal of the "teaching" that willy-nilly occurs on campuses; and if they by no means fully explain the whirlwind that our colleges are currently reaping, they still specify many of the seeds of our present discontent. Most of all, they identify a gulf between our best tradition of policy and our worst contemporary practice that leaves universities open to charges of deficient integrity and a kind of moral laxness which are themselves of an importance that transcends the sheer phenomena of unrest.

If we begin, for example, with our vaunted right of privacy, we must confess that many student resentments with respect to several features of residential life in the academy seem noteworthy mainly in their having been so long in the making. The general quality of dormitory living tends to make ghettoes of student populations, and if the so-called collegial way ever fulfilled its rationale of contributing in a significant fashion to the making of educated men and women, it has clearly deteriorated in our own day to little more than the provision of substandard housing for people enrolled in particular universities. In addition, unlike their noncollege peers, students are frequently subject to unwarranted search and seizure procedures, to restrictions on whom they may visit and whom they may entertain in their living quarters, to the regulation (until very recently) of their dress and personal comportment, and to a host of other inroads on their essentially private conduct. Here as elsewhere, it is not that institutional interference in such matters is entirely without basis in reason and reality; the point is that the interventions have characteristically been made arrogantly, as if they were based on some authoritative right. Seldom has there been a full and direct effort to enlist students in the building of a distinctive community in which the rules reflect some shared ideal; equally seldom has there been a clear and straightforward explanation of the hazards and harassments from the outside that are often elicited or triggered by various forms of student behavior, followed by a search for the common ground on which students and other components of the institution can successfully avert or resist restrictive or repressive forces from the larger society. As a result, it has become easy to perceive the academy as a bit too willing to violate the ethic of civil liberty when its own special concerns are put in jeopardy.

Parenthetically, it should be noted that few faculty members and certainly not many administrative officers have any current, intimate, and sustained awareness of the nature of dormitory life. Understandably, it is a trifle hard to build an accurate image of an institution that cares when the most visible of its official personnel are so preoccupied with other matters that they cannot expose themselves to the conditions under which its largest constituency lives.

Along a somewhat different line, it is difficult to escape the evidence that a kind of double standard operates in our society— one for students and quite another for virtually everybody else. For instance, although they are regularly stimulated by billboards on the main streets and by advertisements in the newspapers of their cities and towns, students are not infrequently barred from producing the plays or showing the films that the larger community obviously supports and at least minimally legitimizes. Similarly, although they have been raised on the rhetoric of a free press, students often find their own journalistic efforts subjected to censorship either blatant or subtle, put under postpublication review that exceeds the usual restraints of press law, or curtailed by rules of editorial eligibility that maximize conventional safety. Again, there may well be reasons for the academic community to conduct itself according to standards that differ from those that have currency beyond its precincts, but the decisions here, to be educative and to reflect institutional commitments to the best traditions of the society in which the American university is embedded, should clearly be made and reviewed within a self-consciously established and maintained ethos of civil liberty.

Even in the intellectual arena, the central room in the academic mansion, the record is seriously smudged. The Velikovsky case represents a startling insistence on orthodoxy from the most distinguished ranks of university-based scientists. In a large number of instances, decisions about professorial hiring, retention, and advancement to tenure have had about them the unfortunate aura of a faculty member's being outside, not the canons of professional, scholarly, and instructional competence, but the limits of disciplinary fashion set by his colleagues. The cost of winning the battles of The Year of the Oath in California was extraordinarily high; the college library is rare that does not have a locked case of books, the circulation of which is restricted on moral or political grounds; and the American Association of University Professors, hardly a radical or impetuous organization, consistently has a score or more of academic freedom cases under review and a dozen institutions on its censured list.

On a somewhat different issue, it is becoming consistently clearer that drug use on campuses is a problem that has civil liberties implications and that must, despite its enormous complexities and difficulties, be dealt with partially in the light of these implications. One can only be morally startled to discover that in eleven of our states, the mandatory penalties for convicted users of marijuana are more severe than those for second-degree murder. Regardless of one's judgments about cannabis and those who smoke it, it is important to remember that pot is neither addictive nor a narcotic and to set this remarkable fact of our laws against another fact: Ours is a drug-using culture. Most of us who are bastions of middle-class uprightness are hooked on the caffein in coffee, tea, and cola drinks, in addition to the aspirin in all our medicine cabinets. (And aspirin is a consciousness-changing agent; it dulls the experience of pain.) We consume huge quantities of tranquilizers; we resort to stimulants like benzedrine often enough to delight the proprietary drug industry, and such is our devotion to alcohol, that original and most widely used of all psychoactive drugs, that it is one of the backbones of our economy. It is also well to bear in mind that we also remain avid consumers of nicotine in spite of the persuasive evidence that it is lethal. When the case is developed in this legitimate direction, it permits a fresh perspective on a problem too often considered as simply a matter of self-indulgence through drug abuse. When the parental generation, including members of the professoriate, inveigh, sometimes over their third predinner cocktail, against the degenerate young who smoke pot, there is some basis for understanding the countercharge of hypocrisy hurled by youth against the established order and for sympathizing with youth's questioning of the legacy of values that has been bequeathed to them. Far beyond the direct issue of the availability and abuse of drugs, the significance of this complex of problems, which define in some crucial respect the ways in which the culture and the nature of the cultural heritage are perceived, cannot be gainsaid or overlooked.

One more illustration: Despite the overwhelmingly liberal rhetoric of academic institutions and academic people with regard to racial questions, universities until very recently (and the changes to date have been extremely small) have behaved in a fashion that suggests that admissions criteria, performance under the modal and common conditions of college instruction, and academic standards of a conventional sort are more valuable than the extension of higher educational opportunity to the disadvantaged. The issues here are genuinely thorny, but it seems reasonable to believe that the actions of our colleges have spoken more loudly than their words on the terrible problems of American race relations. The extent to which reflection about racial questions has been tied to acts and observations by most students is probably not great because of the great gulf which lies between the characteristic experiences of white and black people in the United States.

And this reference to experience calls us to our second large concern, the question of whether universities, no matter how well they may furnish the intellectual opportunities necessary for the examined life, can supply the basis in experience to which ideas can be most effectively related in a developmental sense. Until the civil rights movements of the 1960s, few white, middle-class youth had had any significant and direct dealings with their black counterparts or with the black subculture. As a result, their goodwill was founded on abstractions divorced from concrete relationships and rarely provided any base from which individuals could make sensitive and meaningful decisions about their own responsibilities in this troubled domain of human relations. With student involvement in the civil rights movement, almost the reverse pattern began to take shape. People who acquired intimate awareness of racial injustice, black poverty, and the virulence that white racism often assumes became properly angry and appropriately passionate about the dreadful wrongs of slavery's heritage and the century that began with Reconstruction. But few assimilated that experience intellectually; few have reflected upon the character of their interactions in the South or made sufficient use of ideas to fuse their ardor with sound notions of how to set things right, of how to redeem the damage of our distasteful history. One result is that too little disciplined thought was put into programs for the elimination of poverty and the effective achievement of racial justice; waste, chaos, disappointment, and rancor have too often been the result.

One suspects, for example, that explorations of the concept of justice in our universities must cut more firmly in at least two directions than has been characteristic in our past. On the one hand, our institutions of higher education must come more directly to grips with the question of whether the acceptance of disadvantaged students, regardless of ethnic identity, is at all constructive unless there are adaptations in programs, staff, and standards that will enable these members of the student body to cultivate on terms relevant for them the habits of effective and informed reflection on their own distinctive patterns of experience. It is at least possible that faculty members, socialized through graduate school and committed to careers primarily as scholars, simply do not possess the qualifications to deal with this new clientele in educationally useful ways. Should such prove to be the case, then the problem must be faced of how to enlarge the resources of a university with suitably equipped professors who will not be looked down upon as second-class citizens in the academic republic. In any event, enough is known about the dynamics of learning to lend great weight to the proposition that the increasing diversity of backgrounds and aspirations in contemporary student bodies demands an increasing diversity in the conditions of learning. The two main options of lecture class or seminar may be insufficient to define genuine opportunities for large numbers of the people who come from homes, schools, and social classes that have not before been widely represented on our campuses.

On the other hand, these concerns also demand some extension of the base in experience on which a university education depends. For large numbers of students, mostly white, strong engagement in tutoring, in work in community agencies, in observation in courts and jails, and in becoming familiar through responsible work with the modes of address of city, county, and state governments to racial problems may prove necessary. Perhaps best of all would be the experience of simply living in a black community, sharing as a temporary but still authentic member in its hardships and discovering its resources for joy. For blacks, a comparable increase in experiential familiarity with white society may be equally necessary. On both sides, a careful tying of critical intellectual considerations to the arranged but genuine experiences is essential. The aim is the development of people who can harness their proper passions and their hunger for justice to coherent and potentially meliorative ideas and to notions about how those ideas may be beneficially implemented. The college is serving not as a political mechanism but as a means by which individuals can become more fully human, more deeply committed to the values to which their reflections on their experience may lead them, and more capable of translating their great yearnings into social programs guided by thought.

As it is with the issues of racial justice, so it is with virtually all of the great concepts with which men must toil in their efforts to humanize themselves. The development of the style of the examined life depends on making its base in experience broader and more articulate, on demonstrating the utility of ideas and a disciplined imagination in coping with experience, and on increasing the closeness and the generality of the connections between experience and intellect. Herein lies the potential for transcending the parochialisms of time and place in which so many of us are so dangerously and even tragically locked in a world becoming one and in a time of unprecedentedly rapid change. To achieve this sort of transcendence, the environing ethos of civil liberty seems to be a necessary condition. The dreadful defections from that standard in the past are accusations and warnings; they are not justifications for other ethical and social arrangements which defy this fundamental democratic principle on the ground that, in practice, the principle has frequently been trampled upon.

Within the context of higher education, the proper focus seems clearly to be on personal integration, on the enlargement of social understanding and psychological empathy, on the process by which each man creates for himself new values out of serious reflection on his experience, and on the drawing together of the energizing powers of passion and the critical disciplining and directing potentials of intellect. These objectives define generally the nature of liberal education—a liberating education—for our troubled and crowded time, and our great difficulty lies in achieving these aims on a more widespread and systematic basis than was ever before dreamt of.

That achievement, on a planet where explosive issues of both scale and substance now confront us at virtually every turn, may be a condition of human survival. Our political and social problems are likely to vary at great speed and over a wide range. Our ability to meet them in a humane fashion is likely to depend far less on whether the university politicizes itself in any degree—its doing so, as indicated here, may be either fruitless or destructively self-defeating—than on how well it can facilitate the development of persons who, in their own distinctive ways, live the examined life and thus are able to meet by transcendence the exigencies and trials of convulsive change and to further the most decent impulses of the human animal.

PART

PROCESSES OF CHANGE

TWO

Harold L. Hodgkinson

Walden U.

IV

Most informed critics and champions of higher education would probably agree that we are running low on new ideas. One of the major reasons for this is that we have become preoccupied with existing structures which then blind us from seeing higher education as it might be. Educational functions are being derived from structures, rather than the other way around. One classic function of the visionary is to provide a new model which may have an effect on practice. Without new visions there can be no new alternatives.

Evidence for the failure of higher education is all around us. If technology consists of those devices which make it unnecessary for us to experience the world, then education has become tech-

This paper appeared in *Soundings, An Interdisciplinary Journal,* 1969, *52*(2).

nological. Many of our brightest students are telling us that higher education is insulating them from reality rather than assisting them to peel off its infinite layers. We know also that many of the faculty, old men by the age of forty, are having their own identity crises, and the large number of early presidential retirements and resignations suggests that all is not well in the administrative camp either. Much of this disaffection comes from the preoccupation of higher education with structure and its inability to deal seriously with process. The notion that human beings are capable of being educated without a vast array of numbers, letters, times, and compartments is anathema to many educators, who seem to share Machiavelli's dictum that "unless men are compelled to be good they will invariably turn out to be bad."[1]

Americans tend to feel uncomfortable in discussions of process. Early discussion of this chapter has indicated that collaboration, trust, and growth are a part of the educational rhetoric but not a part of the educational scene. If we wish to make reality out of rhetoric, we must adopt the view that structures are potentially evil, and that the goal is not a maximum of structure, but the absolute minimum without which the institution could not survive. Heavily structured colleges tend to graduate people who have been subjected to these institutional controls but who have not developed much in the way of private, personal control structures. (Or as one wag put it, small Christian colleges make small Christians.) This chapter is an attempt to develop a new conception of a college in which process and individuality predominate, and structure and system are seen as means to individualistic ends.

Certain assumptions are basic to my proposal: First, learning does not occur in equal units, nor on certain days of the week, nor at certain times of day. When it does occur, it means that the individual's view of the world has shifted; learning is additive. Second, when twenty students read the same book, they have twenty different experiences. Third, transfer of learning outcomes from one situation to another is highly unlikely. It is wiser to assume that transfer will not happen. Fourth, the universe does not seem to be

[1] *The Prince* (New York: Crofts Classics), p. 71.

organized by academic departments. Fifth, a good educational program provides for the personal growth of faculty and administrators as well as students. Sixth, the present status and mobility systems of the professoriat are un- if not anti-intellectual. Seventh, the job of certifying people for jobs in the meritocracy should be moved off campus and into state agencies in which performance criteria will be established. Eighth, administrative positions and committees often have the function of generating enough work to justify their continued existence. Ninth, the rigid lines between content and method, teacher and student, ignorance and knowledge, and teaching and research need to be made more interactive and processual. Tenth, participation in governance should be direct, not representative, and should include all interested parties. Eleventh, standing committees, and the precedents which they enshrine, are major causes of the hardening of institutional arteries. Twelfth, a student body should not be age-graded, but should be limited to those who wish to inquire about something. Inquiry transcends sex, age, nationality, and social class. Thirteenth, one of the richest forms of education involves imitation. Through imitation can come identification with the personality and values of the person imitated. Finally, cultural deprivation is not limited to the lower class —in many respects, middle-class children know far less about the universe of humanity than do others.

Basic to the entire program is the concept of inquiry. Inquiry is the bridge between teaching and learning, content and method, as seen in the ninth assumption. Pedagogy, therefore, comes to mean the act of mutual inquiry. This means the virtual elimination of all formal teaching as such; no grades, no courses, no diplomas. The basic work unit consists of the faculty member working with students in a research mode. (This is a very loose definition of research—any investigation or inquiry process would suffice, if mutually agreeable.)

The student will probably take a broader view of the investigation than the faculty member; therefore, the students will be able to form linkages between and around the more specific interests of the faculty. It is through this linkage that the basis of general education could be built. Although the student may come to Walden with only one area of inquiry in his mind, his associations with others should begin to expand his interests—after all, everyone will be excited about his learning, and will want to communicate it, and some "conversions" will probably be made. Because students will be drawn from all age groups and all economic backgrounds (there need be few barriers to admission), the possibilities of general education through human contacts should be enhanced. To borrow an old idea, the student's education through human contacts should be seen as an inverted pyramid, coming into Walden with one area of interest and realizing that it is interrelated with thousands of others.

In a collaborative model such as this, the lines between teacher and student will become blurred; since most students know more about some things than faculty do and no evaluation of the student's worth would be required, both would be free to learn from each other. They would have nothing to lose by doing so, and both could gain simultaneously. Age-grading will be very difficult in this environment, in that many of the students will be older than the faculty. The faculty may be more theoretically astute but a student group representing all ages and diverse backgrounds could bring a rich experiential base from which to validate and inform theoretical perspectives. Although the initial period of Walden will probably result in student imitation of and identification with faculty, a reversal may well set in if status distinctions between faculty and students can be kept at a minimal level.

Because the curriculum is conceived in terms of process, its only visible presence would be the areas of inquiry which each faculty member posts on his door. Technically these areas are not the curriculum but only the arenas in which the inquiry processes operate. All will be free to work individually or in groups, but no group activity will come about without the expressed agreement of the group that it is desirable. (Participants can meet for an hour or a year, shifting memberships as needed. It is clear that if they have to meet for an hour every week, they will think of something to do, but then the time unit would be determining the activity, as

DeGrazia observed[2]). Every attempt will be made to keep group behavior as flexible as possible, in terms of both duration of meetings and ease of entering and leaving groups. These work groups should look like a kaleidoscope of shifting group patterns, as the system is here subordinated to the task, contrary to the conventional norm which makes tasks subordinate to system. Most of the systematization of curriculum is necessary only because of the institution's obligation to certify to the outside world that a student has passed through a certain number of hours and units of exposure and can be certified; if the certification function is eliminated, most of the curricular systems are automatically eliminated at the same time.

Although there will be no common texts (see our second assumption), there will be an attempt to develop experiential bases for looking at student growth. Unlike much current theory, Walden will operate on the notion that human personality development does not occur in a series of fixed, immutable stages, each one necessary for passage to the next. Rather the person will be seen as having flexible access to many growth-inducing stimuli at any time, in any environment. Human growth is seen as a lifelong process, not a phenomenon of childhood and adolescence ending at age twenty-one. The student will be encouraged to plan experiences which will result in growth along certain major dimensions (see below, the Walden rationale). In that there is no generation gap to these dimensions, they will be as relevant to faculty growth as to students. Because of the elimination of the certification function, students and faculty will be encouraged to develop valid *self*-perceptions of their progress along experiential lines that they have chosen. This sort of self-evaluation is a vital part of the process network of Walden, and faculty should serve as role models for students in terms of self-appraisals of growth and change. Good teachers have always been able to make use of the fact that different people perceive phenomena differently, but in the research-inquiry context of Walden, these differences can be made even clearer and more productive.

Many materials will be available as support services for in-

[2] S. DeGrazia, *Of Time, Work and Leisure* (New York: Twentieth Century Fund, 1962).

quiry. When tools such as math or statistics, formal logic, a foreign language, or research design are needed, they will be available in programmed form. In the present pattern students usually take these courses before they have need for them and must brush up on the material before they can put it to use. In Walden they will learn it as they need it. There is no particular reason to assume that any time will be lost in this plan; in fact, knowledge gained and put to immediate use may stay with the learner for a longer period of time. These tools will be seen as means to ends; no claim will be made that they build character or are a part of the Western heritage.

However, the arts and crafts will have a strong place in the activities at Walden, for there is much evidence that experience in the arts can be important for the development of the dimensions listed in the Walden rationale, below. There will be few professional artists in Walden, but everyone will be encouraged to develop his own modes of artistic expression. Again, the faculty will be models in this area, and the words *amateur* and *dilettante* will be the highest compliment rather than the lowest insult.

Because the output of Walden will not have to be certified, the student input also escapes the need for codification and certification. The great virtue of Walden lies in the possibility of mixing very different people together to learn from each other in a situation of low or no threat. The fifty-year-old Mexican gardener, anxious to discover the roots and nature of prejudice, would be very welcome even if he had completed only six years of schooling. Virtually anyone who wishes to engage in inquiry could be admitted, for admission is not seen as a guarantee of anything. The student can stay for a day or ten years, and fees would be prorated on a daily basis and determined by ability to pay. Because of the flexibility of the program, the student body will not have to be carefully regulated as to size. The goal will be to let in as many people as possible, rather than to keep as many out as possible (it is estimated that of those who apply to institutions of higher education, only one in twenty graduates; clearly one of the latent functions of higher education is to make most people feel rejected). Because of the desire to attract all races and social classes, as well as all age levels, Walden will probably not be residential, for students will be living active lives in addition to being involved at Walden. In fact, there need not be a central campus, as permanent buildings make for permanent programs. Modern communications systems would make it possible for Walden to exist all over a large urban area, bringing the campus to the community rather than the other way around.

No one will graduate from Walden; he will leave. A possible substitute for graduation could be the celebration which would come from the completion of a task of inquiry. After some festivities, the teachers and students responsible would present the results of their inquiry as a gift to the school. Several hundred such events could be held each year, ranging through all the areas of human inquiry. This is probably the only group teaching that will occur at Walden, and might represent in its entirety a fair approach to general education. There will be no finality to these celebrations, since it is assumed that inquiry never ends. But the community can be happy that the process has reached a given stage. Such parties would also be good places for the faculty and students to sing and dance together. Although our stereotypes about thinking would lead us to believe that Walden would be a grim place (thinking is hard, dangerous, and depressing, as it is for Hamlet) the realities of people coming together to share and celebrate could make a real community out of Walden.

One of the most difficult tasks will be that of debriefing entering students in terms of their highly structured expectations of academic life and their probable inability to engage in autonomous, self-directed work. This will require the best efforts of a highly skilled person, referred to later as the psycho-social registrar. It is most likely that the more mature entering student (in terms of age) will have some advantage in this regard, and the younger students may emulate the more self-directed patterns of the older ones. Even the person who is vague as to the areas he wishes to inquire about can try them out for a week or a month and stop whenever he wishes, with no penalty or punishment.

The normal relationship between size of student body and institutional income will not hold in Walden, for the duplication of construction which provides for classrooms, residence halls, faculty office space, and research facilities can be avoided. A rough approximation of size of student body at any given time would be five hundred. On grounds of ability to pay, fees could range from $50 to $9,000 per year, broken down into daily equivalents. With a mean tuition of $4,000, one could pay a faculty of one hundred an average salary of $14,000 a year and still have $600,000 left for operating expenses. It is to be expected that about half the faculty members' time could be paid for through research grants, thus saving Walden another $700,000. There would be no conflict of interest here, since the faculty member teaches through his research activities. No faculty load statistics would have to be calculated; there is no assumption that the faculty are identical, interchangeable parts. Some may have twenty students working with them, while others may work with only one or two. Student scholarship assistance would be written into grant proposals for research and clerical assistants.

It is hoped that this arrangement would have a significant impact on the faculty reward and status systems of increasing the importance of qualitative evaluations and decreasing the importance of quantitative ones. Number of students, size of research grants, number of publications, and the like would be of little use within the Walden community, for there would be no promotional hierarchy in which these would be used. This would be tough country in which to try to build an empire. There would be no reason for tenure, and no point in splitting the faculty into junior and senior levels, with the juniors trying to climb into the senior bag. The conventional faculty reward system is extraneous to the person. With adequate financing, Walden could help faculty to develop intrinsic rewards which would be more meaningful.

Walden will illustrate the dictum that the best government is the least government. First, there will be no positions without clearly defined tasks which are ascertained from the title. This means that there will be no president, and no dean. (After all, what are the things that presidents and deans do? The titles do not clarify the activities.) A variant of Parkinson's First Law—positions generate work which must be done to justify the position—will be used to keep down the number of administrative tasks. Fund-raising, which is usually considered to be in the province of the President, will be contracted to an outside firm, just as one can contract for food service, dormitory construction and supervision, and so forth. The fund-raising agency will appoint a board of supporters. They will be responsible to the agency, not the college, and will be selected for their ability to give and get money for the college. They will have no influence at all on the governance of Walden, but they will receive a 5 per cent commission on every dollar they raise for Walden. The profit motive has worked well for these people in the past, and the conditioned reflex of working hard for profit may make this board more effective than some others.

Although there will be no vertical hierarchy of positions in Walden, one person will be the most visible. He is the coordinator of inquiry. Elected by the students and faculty for a three-year renewable term, he will serve as a communication link of the first magnitude, and should represent the best characteristics of mind and personality in Walden. He will most likely be a faculty member, but because the student body is not age-graded, a student could also be elected. Hopefully, he will be able to continue his own inquiry on a reduced basis, if he is wise enough to avoid self-generating tasks which must be continued after their first performance. In that there will be no standing committees, and precedent will not be determinative, the decision on the machinery to be used will be made by him for each individual case. The one assumption that should guide him would be that of involving as many concerned members of Walden as possible, conceivably everyone who wishes to get involved. He can be recalled by a two-thirds vote of the student-faculty body.

The coordinator of inquiry will be responsible for making two crucial appointments. The first is that of manager of finance and auxiliaries. He will oversee the functions of accounting and disbursement of funds, food service, buildings and grounds, and equipment purchase. Although the manager is selected by the coordinator of inquiry, he can also be recalled by a two-thirds vote. Business managers often have a very influential role in academic policy decisions, since they sit in high councils where such things are discussed. In that there will be no high councils at Walden, the influence of the manager of finance will be limited to his own vote in community decision-making.

The coordinator's most important appointment will be that of the last member of the administration, the psycho-social registrar. Although his formal power will be low, his attitude and personal skills will be crucial to the success of the program. He will be a skilled psychometrician, well trained in counselling and testing in all its phases. At the time of admission, all new faculty and students will have an extended interview with the psycho-social registrar, at which time some agreement on the person's goals for his stay in Walden will be reached, and some attempt at setting up criteria for personal growth will be made. After this initial interview, all further contacts will be at the request of the individual faculty member or student. In that the coordinator will have absolutely no ability to threaten or coerce, it is to be hoped that he would become very busy with individuals who wish to develop their ability to understand themselves, and to assess their personal and intellectual growth. In that Walden will not be a certifying agency, these confidential records will be given to the person when he leaves, rather than being kept at the college. It may be that a group at Walden will wish some assessment of their work, but the matter of personal confidentiality of all records of growth will be the responsibility of the psycho-social registrar. He also will have to know the current interests of faculty and students so that he can steer the new student in the best direction. In that the ability to assess one's personal and intellectual growth is a prime objective of Walden, the registrar probably teaches the most important skills of anyone at Walden. He must be extremely broad in his interests so that he can help people translate the results of their inquiries into personal growth and development. Like the manager, the psycho-social registrar can be recalled by a two-thirds vote of the student-faculty group.

Every effort will be made to avoid the establishment of an elaborate committee structure. Most problems will arise in the context of the work of faculty and students, and should be solved at that level. Problems which have a broader level of application will be communicated to the coordinator of inquiry, who will establish the procedures for the handling of that particular problem. By minimizing precedent and abolishing standing committees, it is fervently hoped that the widely noted tendency of faculty members to play politics will be reduced if not eliminated. By making administrative tasks as clear as possible, and by reducing the vertical status hierarchy which provides ego massage and political sophistication for many administrators, the administration may truly find their rewards in serving the needs of others.

There are many advantages to Walden as a concept, such as the genuine student mix, the elimination of vertical hierarchies, the possibility of moving this institution into an area of hard-core poverty and working through people of the area who could not be rejected by the school, and the specificity of administrative roles. There obviously would be problems as well. One of these concerns the faculty member who wants to leave Walden and return to the more conventional reward system of other colleges and universities. His re-entry might well be painful in terms of position and salary if the other institution failed to recognize the worth of what he had done at Walden. He also would find it extremely difficult to adjust to the highly structured situation of most university faculty members. There is no easy answer to this. However, it would seem that the faculty who learned how to work well in the Walden setting would probably become a superb teacher in almost any collegiate setting. His research, freed from the political compulsions of keeping up with the minute and the mundane, might reach a greater level of significance. Another problem concerns the tendency for Walden to fill up with those interested in social and scientific areas, leaving the arts and humanities behind. It may be that the professional artists or humanists would not be too interested in Walden, but it is clearly assumed that faculty members would for the most part have active roles in the arts and humanities as amateurs. It also might be that Walden would fill up with professional students, who want to spend their whole lives there. This, of course, happens now at almost every university. The only defense would be that Walden would make the rest of the world look more interesting rather than less; it would hardly be a good place for a recluse. Most students and faculty would be off campus as much as on, pursuing their inquiry wherever it led. The psycho-social registrar could act in severe cases of student and faculty inability to grow and develop in the Walden environment, but such cases would be rare. The registrar will admit anyone unless he can prove a case against them, and after admission it will be assumed that they are being productive unless there is evidence to the contrary.

One final question is whether or not there are people capable of working productively in a place like this. The answer is that new visions must by definition depend more on the human potential than the conventional modes. Thus far, the evidence would suggest that the human creature is infinitely more capable than our social structures will allow him to be.

The conventional college experience forces the student to concentrate on those things which he can do well and which are a part of the reward and certification system of the institution. This approach, called variously "psyching out the institution" and "leading from strength," is bound to result in an individual with narrow insight into his potential. Because of the meritocratic sword hanging over him, he is not allowed to dabble, to fail, or even to be casual. As Riesman puts it, "Leading from strength may rob the students of the possibility of discovering other areas in which they may not be so well-equipped, but which may nevertheless be more relevant for them as they slowly grow."[3] It could be argued that faculty are forced into a view of themselves which is very similar in its narrowness to that of the student, that "leading from weakness" may be the most important strategy for personal growth, yet our institutions of higher education, because of their obligation (self-imposed) to evaluate and judge human worth, cannot allow this to happen.

A theory of human development which successfully integrates the individual and the social structures in which he participates has yet to be created. It certainly does not seem to be on the horizon at the moment. Perhaps closest is the work of Stern[4] and others (based on Murray)[5] which tries to relate individual needs to the "press" imposed on the individual by the institution. But this

[3] Personal communication.

[4] G. Stern, *People in Context* (New York: Wiley, 1969).

[5] H. Murray, *Explorations in Personality* (New York: Oxford University Press, 1938).

is not a longitudinal theory, and does not help us to explain or predict how different individuals will grow through similar structures in different ways.

Because of this failure, we are forced to the position of simply trying to keep the doors to new experience as open as possible. The best metaphor for how this can be done is the system of scrambled access cafeteria patterns. In previous systems, it was assumed that everyone had to enter at the same place, go all the way through the line, and emerge at the other end. In the scrambled system, there is no line. Each person simply goes to the various staging areas to get what he wants, in the order he wants. This metaphor could apply to the passage through college as well as through a cafeteria line—in a normal college program, all the students move through a heavily structured line, picking up items in the order imposed by the institution (course A must be taken before course B). The line never varies, so the students cannot vary. A scrambled access curriculum, based on the principle that the learner selects his own sequence of experiences as he perceives a need for them, could be defended both in terms of efficiency and in terms of what is known about personality development.

For example, the conventional cafeteria line curriculum is designed to allow invidious comparisons to be made between middle-class and lower-class students (the line structure certainly favors the middle-class student, and giving the lower-class student more time to get into the line does not change the essential fact that the line was not designed with his needs, skills, and values in mind). In the scrambled access model, invidious comparisons would be almost impossible, for there would be no standard route, which all would take and which would allow for rating individual performance of identical tasks. Age-grading would also be impossible, as there would be no relation of student age to his work (in the conventional curricular cafeteria, those who enter the line are the young; those who leave are the old). Similarly, little emphasis would be placed on one-way theories of personality development, with their usual insistence that one stage must be handled before the next can be reached. In that there is no personality theory which successfully takes us through all of Shakespeare's stages of man, we will assume that the adult is still full of growth potential, and that it is not necessarily unhealthy to be forty and still not know what you want to be "when you grow up." Because no one knows what directions of growth are typical of adults, there is no justification for any linear or sequenced system, and the scrambled access approach remains superior in terms of maximizing personal growth.

The best way to achieve a scrambled access curricular model is through a research-inquiry scheme like that of Walden. The student can move into (not through) it at any points he wishes; he continues to be free to move in new directions at any time, and to move in several different directions simultaneously. Just as pluralism remains as the bedrock of a healthy democracy, so the pluralistic principle is the best approach to understanding the complex interweaving of factors which constitutes an individual personality.

John David Maguire

Strategies for Academic Reform

V

Change does not necessarily assure progress, but progress implacably requires change.[1]

Of course we shall have to make the future, for no one else is in charge here.[2]

"There is more to the business of producing beneficial change than passion and provocation, frustration and fury,"[3] *yet even when one*

[1] H. S. Commager, "Change in History," *Freedom and Order: A Commentary on the American Political Scene* (New York: Braziller, 1966), p. 244.

[2] W. Moore, "The Utility of Utopias," *American Sociological Review,* 1966, *31*(6), 767.

[3] E. D. Etherington, President's Matriculation Address, Wesleyan University, September 15, 1968.

knows where There is, the hardest human problem is getting from Here to There.

This chapter explores some principles that inform sound, effective academic change and the strategies and tactics that these principles suggest. Axioms, even axioms for change, often sound abstract and empty and run the risk, in Trow's words, of "inexpensive moralizing which banters about institutional realities in the name of high principle and results in irrelevant prescriptions to imaginary universities with real names."[4] Without attention to strategies for change the chapters on goals in this volume might be vulnerable to such a charge. Even this chapter, with its examination of very concrete processes of academic reform, runs the risks of emptiness and insufficient specificity, especially because of its formalism. The formalism results from our dealing with a style for academic reform rather than with its substance. Our concern here is with the way change is effected and not with the content of change. The formalism has been consciously adopted in the effort to argue that any major change—ill as well as good, regressive as well as progressive, conservative as well as liberal—could be achieved by pursuing these strategies and tactics. Birchers, radicals, and all reformers in between might be most likely to succeed in securing the adoption of their programs by employing these strategies. The strategies are, in this sense only, neutral and can be used in the realization of the widest variety of goals. Thus they are analogous to formal axioms.

In the effort to avoid complete emptiness and an irrelevance of complete abstractness, however, we make frequent reference to points in other chapters—some which buttress our argument, others which provide concrete examples, and still others which run counter to our counsel and so pose a challenge.

Ideally, changes in educational program and function should be going on continuously, if gradually and undramatically. In fact,

[4] M. Trow, "Conceptions of the University," *The American Behavioral Scientist,* 1968, *11*(5), 14–21.

however, educational changes seem to occur by fits and starts, as Charles Muscatine wrote of Berkeley, "through shocks of drastic adjustment following periods of quiescence."[5] Shock waves, now commonplace on countless campuses, signal the end of quiescence at these institutions.

In the week this chapter was completed (May 7–14, 1969) students and police battled for three nights in Madison, Wisconsin, exchanging rocks and tear gas after students tried to hold a block party without a permit. At Chicago a radical sociology professor was almost beaten to death in his office. At Dartmouth forty students were given thirty-day jail sentences, and fined $100 each, on criminal contempt charges, after they refused to obey a court order to leave the administration building during an ROTC protest. At Howard in Washington, D.C., federal deputies fired tear gas into dormitories and arrested twenty-six students occupying six buildings who had said they wanted to make the curriculum relevant to the black community. At City College of New York arsonists set fire to the student center, and black students who wanted to keep the campus closed (to win demands for more nonwhite enrollment) battled with white students who wanted to go to class. Two weeks before, black students occupying a building in an effort to get demands met at Cornell had armed themselves on hearing that white fraternity men were planning to force them out. Berkeley continued to engage in its annual quota of disruption, and venerable Harvard erupted in the spring. The rate of student protest grew to the point that most newspapers carried daily front page thumbnail accounts of disruptions much like baseball box scores.

A principal source of protests is the widespread feeling that universities no longer have students as their primary concern. Highly touted institutions which promise so much to so many have increasingly given too little to too few, and now the chickens are coming home to roost. "People suffering from institutions that can't respond, problems that are virtually left untouched, and the myriad uncertainties of their own private and public existence must in-

[5] C. Mucatine, *Education at Berkeley: Report of the Select Committee on Education* (Berkeley: University of California, 1966), p. 4.

evitably rise in protest. . . . Frustration breeds anger, . . . a demand for change, coupled with an increasing dislike and contempt for those responsible for the present."[6]

In the wake of crisis, the makers of change—whether trustees, administrators, or faculty—hurry through some mollifying alterations which they hope will be an improvement (but are often soon shown not to be).

Here is an instance where fact can illumine ideal; it leads to our first principle: Since change is "occasioned," the time flow of an institution should be envisaged as a series of occasions, each to be made the most of. The university, like few other social institutions, lives by symbols. Symbolic actions count heavily there and what the university suggests by its actions in a given moment, on a given occasion, is often the vehicle for change. And while every occasion is crucial, it need not be critical.

A change in the university presidency is often such an occasion. A new president usually begins with a fund of goodwill and high campus morale. If he is willing to spend his goodwill capital early, he can often persuade colleagues to perceive new horizons and work toward them, achieving far more innovation at the outset of his administration than will be possible later on. For a variety of reasons college and university presidents are resigning at an unprecedented pace, provoking one faculty member to counsel a colleague under consideration for a presidency that given their brevity of tenure and the rate of turnover, you could accept a presidency and hardly interrupt your scholarly career. At this writing, eighty-four major presidencies are unfilled.

The departure in midcareer of a key administrator or senior professor can be another such occasion. Having reached an impasse locally, but having laid the ground work for significant future strides, the departing administrator or professor may, in a series of parting shot actions or statements, catalyze positive change.

Rather than being viewed as threats, the impingement on the university of social movements—antimilitarism, group consciousness, concern about economic disparities within America and the world—

[6] R. Goodwin, "Sources of the Public Unhappiness," *The New Yorker,* 1969, *44*(46), p. 44.

may be made the occasion for a fundamental rethinking of the purposes of the university. In 1969, the specific concerns were the war in Vietnam and the university's putative complicity in it, racism in American society and in university policy, the minimal role of students in governing the university, the continuing irrelevance of too many courses, the declining quality of the environment, and overpopulation.

These extra-academic happenings that originate outside the university and move within are generally nonprogrammed and unplanned. In Richard Wertz's chapter on the introduction of the social inquiry program at MIT, he makes clear that events outside the university first led to the formation and development of a protest community within MIT. Then came the completely unforeseen taking of sanctuary there by an AWOL soldier. Wertz wrote: "We have often jokingly said that MIT's sanctuary [of an AWOL soldier] was our best social and educational event. MIT was galvanized as never before by this protest. . . . The value of this . . . extra-structural community happening was that everyone involved learned something about his university and himself that would bear fruit in later months."

Picking up the rhythm of the times and stimulated by these developments in its environing society, the university may generate new policies and programs that unite intellectual activity on the campus with life in the wider world in wiser, healthier ways.

The fact that such impingements often manifest themselves in stormy campus confrontations need not foreclose the possibility of sound, new programs emerging in their wake. It is important to note, however, that the form of some occasions prevents the subsequent development of healthy programs. Oak trees cannot grow from dandelion seeds. A Third World College cannot be housed in a building burned to the ground in the effort to dramatize the need for such a college.

The key to constructive responses to impinging social movements lies in anticipating and working with them. A simple, but fundamental way of doing this—gracefully employed by the MIT administration when challenged by the group developing the social inquiry program—is to provide those demanding reform with adequate means and resources to publicly state their position. (In the MIT case this meant granting a part-time secretary, an office, mailing privileges, reproducing privileges, and one-third time off for a faculty coordinator.) A reform position must ultimately win its way in the open market. Avoiding the suppression of its statement—and even the appearance of suppression—and, indeed, encouraging its getting a fair hearing is a basic way to amicable change. When this occurs, societal impingements may provide an occasion for forging new unions between thought and experience, thus rendering intellectual inquiry more responsible.

This model reverses the understanding of an institution's life as a kind of undifferentiated timeless continuum. It views it instead as a series of related moments—each full of challenges and opportunities as well as threats and dangers. While encouraging experiment and the risk of change, such an understanding reinforces the need for the university to be a change-criticizing as well as a change-creating institution. Since policies and programs are elicited by and for a given time—five years, ten, even fifteen—they must be regularly appraised, and dissolved when their day is done. An institution that views its development as a series of moments attempts to monitor as well as maximize those moments.

To restate our first principle: An academic institution is much more likely to effect changes in its educational program and function if its members view its development as a series of occasions or possibility-filled moments.

Politics, in the richest sense, is the process through which change is achieved. All political movements are efforts to redistribute power and reshape the ways it is shared and exercised. Hence our second principle: Academic change requires new alliances among those who constitute the university, that is, new patterns within established constituencies as well as recognition of new or overlooked constituencies.

From World War II until recently the faculty has been the key constituency in the fashioning of academic reform. And within the faculty, departmental logrolling has been the standard device for intrafaculty alliance and institutional change. The situation is now rapidly shifting. Major changes within the faculty's province—

curriculum, academic regulations, new academic programs, the university calendar, and so forth—are increasingly achieved through coalitions of professors who agree on an issue somewhat independently of their departmental affiliations—a phenomenon not unlike recent studies of religious communions (for example, Gerhard Lenski's *The Religious Factor*[7]) that show that liberals within, say, Judaism are more like Protestant and Catholic liberals than like conservatives within Judaism itself. The MIT experience described by Wertz is a perfect example of such a coalition. From the outset faculty of varied disciplines have been involved and at each point where formal voting was required a majority of faculty in a number of fields carried the day. These cross-departmental ideological alliances are appearing with greater frequency and are the key to academic reform within the faculty. This new form of intraconstituency alliance is characteristic—and will have to be so increasingly—of each of the other groups we shall mention.

This principle, when applied to faculty, further implies that the effective unit for academic change is no longer, if it ever was, the isolated professor but is a group or team. Goodwin Watson comments on the importance of a colleague group both for the content of a new program and for the politics of its passage: "The campus team is the most desirable unit for change. Members of the collaborative team can improve the design of a project because each has insights that others lack. They can forge a cohesive unit of mutual support. The resistance of the old guard will not disappear, but a team is not so safe a target as is a single deviate person."[8]

Students, meanwhile, are becoming much more directly and officially involved in the processes of making institutional decisions. They have now become a political constituency and as such must be viewed by members of the other university constituencies as potential formal allies.

[7] G. Lenski, *The Religious Factor* (Garden City, N.Y.: Doubleday, 1961).

[8] G. Watson, "Reward Systems for Innovation," a paper presented to Section 22 at the 24th National Conference on Higher Education, sponsored by the American Association for Higher Education, Chicago, March 4, 1969, p. 3.

Adminstrators, long the expediters of change, are often initiators of reform as well. But the restraints on their freedom to function as change agents are very great indeed. Because of this fact many administrators are inclined to plead their roles as brokers in explanation of the slowness of reform on their campuses. While some administrators overestimate their capacity for initiating reform, most underestimate their powers, unsure whether to play a role or be a man.

Perhaps the most overlooked group in analyses of academic reform are members of the governing board—trustees or regents. The findings of the recent nationwide study of trustees by the Educational Testing Service[9] coupled with the notorious performance of the Regents of the University of California might well chill hopes of finding trustees sympathetic to positive change. However, JB Lon Hefferlin's national study of change in higher education revealed that most major academic reforms at the institutions he studied were supported and pushed by board members, and most of them would not have occurred had it not been for board action. He declared: "We would suggest that the governing board, more than any other unit of the institution, must be held responsible for assuring the continuity of academic reform. By its selection of the president, its setting of a level of aspiration for the institution, its efforts at financial support, its supervision of the budget, and its role as the continuous overseer of the institution, the board can assure a climate for educational change more powerfully than any other group of its members."[10]

Evidence mounts that the constituency most resistant to major academic reforms is not the trustees or regents, but the faculty.[11] James Rust recently declared: "On most campuses the greatest abusers of power and the hardest people to get at are the

[9] *College and University Trustees: Their Backgrounds, Roles and Educational Attitudes: A Survey* (Princeton: Educational Testing Service, 1969).

[10] JB L. Hefferlin, *Dynamics of Academic Reform* (San Francisco: Jossey-Bass, 1969), pp. 44–45.

[11] See C. Jencks and D. Riesman, *The Academic Revolution* (New York: Doubleday, 1968) and M. Ways, "The Faculty Is the Heart of the Trouble," *Fortune*, 1969, *79*(1).

faculty. I don't think there is anything in the world as conservative as a university faculty. I don't think there is anything as hard to move when it comes to their own interests."[12] Goodwin Watson makes the same point: "When we think of the faculty member and educational innovation, the image that comes to my mind is a balky mule. He is resolutely immobile, obstinate, obdurate, and refractory. He is stuck in a rut, intractable and impervious. To move him one must cajole or threaten, bribe or prod. Is that fantasy at all appropriate to our colleagues or ourselves?"[13]

One explanation for this resistance to change may be the way in which guild or bloc mentality has reinforced self-interest, especially since 1950. Harold Hodgkinson reports that in a recent nationwide study of campus constituencies, in which 1,232 faculty members were questioned, the educational problem most often cited was "keeping class sizes small." The number two problem was "class scheduling and teaching load." The problem of the quality of teaching ranked seventh. Faculty are shown by the study to be perhaps the most self-interested group in the university and the group least willing to decide matters from the perspective of the entire institution.[14]

Surprisingly, trustees may be the least self-interested members of the university, aware of the widest range of campus concerns. Students often mistakenly make them the target of their primary attacks when, in fact, trustees are often much more sensitive to the need for rapid educational change than faculty. The failure of students to seek allies among the trustees is a major reason why efforts at reform in so many institutions die at birth.

Jencks and Riesman, in their matter-of-fact way, declare: "The young can no more afford to go their own way independent of adults than Ghana or Cuba can get on without help from at least some of the great powers."[15] Whatever one thinks of the politics of

[12] Quoted in J. Brann, "The Campus Ombudsman," *Chronicle of Higher Education,* 1968, *3*(5), 4.

[13] Watson, *loc. cit.,* p. 1.

[14] H. Hodgkinson, "Governance and Factions—Who Decides Who Decides?" *The Research Reporter,* The Center for Research and Development in Higher Education, 1968, *3*(3), pp. 5–6.

[15] Jencks and Riesman, *loc. cit.,* p. 60.

the metaphor, the point is true regarding academic reform. No single constituency within the university—students, faculty, administration, trustees—can achieve change alone. Schwartz's chapter in this volume, which romantically inflates the role and power of students in achieving change and trumpets a "We must go it alone" attitude, is on this score patently wrong.

Attempts at reform outside the university as well as within have frequently floundered because the pioneers leading them failed to forge alliances with members of other groups who, though less stringent in their perceptions than the pioneers and less strident in their proclamations, were nevertheless in a position to materially effect the realization of the reform. Trustees may, in this sense, prove invaluable mediators between the institution and its wider environment as well as allies and agents for change within the institution.

A glance at the burgeoning black studies programs around the country clearly illustrates this point. Although calls for such programs typically began with students and a few faculty, those programs that have been adopted and the considerably fewer now in operation have resulted from alliances with adminstrators and approval by trustees. Programs are not funded and solidly established until such alliances are formed. Because of hostility toward the administration, many such programs are paradoxically much less imaginative than they would have been had administrators been allowed to participate in their planning. It appears that a unified approach to the creation of black studies programs is infinitely more desirable than simply combining pieces from already existing departments and reinforcing the reigning disciplines. But this approach is rarely achieved without administrative support and its adoption can rarely be gained without alliances between key members of all university constituencies. Wherever a plan for university change originates, its advocates must seek support in as many quarters as possible—even those that historically have been thought distant and unlikely allies. Without new coalitions that transcend old constituency politics, significant educational reform cannot occur.

In his illuminating book, *Dynamics of Academic Reform,*

Hefferlin cites "circulation" as the primary key to educational change.[16] By circulation he means the movement or lack of movement (actual and in attitudes) among and within institutions. He explores change of persons—the replacement and rotation of individuals, the introduction of new individuals—as well as change in persons—alterations in attitudes and skills—as major instruments of circulation and notes the university's excessive reliance on the former for stimulating academic reform. He declares that the rate of academic change tends to vary with the rate of turnover in personnel. Encouragingly, we sense that turnover is not as fundamental a mechanism for reform as we had pessimistically suspected it might be, but we sense that it remains the major mechanism for instituting and implementing major academic realignments in an institution.

Hefferlin's study provides the background for our third principle: Important changes in educational program occur where there is already internal movement in the institution. As in a healthy human body, so in a sound academic institution, lively circulation must be maintained and encouraged. The ability to change is not a function of the age of an institution. Some of the oldest are the liveliest, while some of the youngest are the most inhibited—a fact also often seen in the contrast between families with several generations of wealth and the new rich. The former are secure enough to gamble while the latter dare not risk their recently achieved, still precarious station. That is why, spiritually and institutionally speaking, the rich and the very poor get richer. Both groups are confident or reckless enough to dare. The rich can afford to risk an occasional loss; the poor cannot lose. The most serious obstacles to change afflict institutions from their outset, and the youngest are as vulnerable as the oldest. These obstacles are pessimism, insecurity, futility, limited resources, and ideological restrictions. As an institution grows older, the weight of tradition may itself become an obstacle, but it is probably not nearly so impeding as the bureaucratic restraints that may develop early, that is, excessive requirements for coordination and the centralization of initiative or institutional power.

[16] *Op. cit.*

Change itself stimulates health. And those institutions are healthiest that continue to attract fresh blood while challenging the people already there to keep moving in new ways. The fundamental problem in the future will be to prompt change in attitudes and work styles among the permanent, established members of the institution. Institutional renewal will not take place without renewal in outlook and commitment on the part of those within the institution. Producing change in adults is a deep mystery and profound challenge which simply must be met.

Effective communication within an institution is at the heart of sound growth. Sometimes the withholding of information within parts of the university is purposeful. When the information is important, withholding it leads to serious conflict. More often, the bad habit of secretiveness simply triumphs, with no less grievous results. For example, few practices can stimulate involvement throughout an institution as much as opening its treasurer's books, disclosing its financial situation, and allowing campus-wide review of its fiscal policies. The gains in honest understanding, in the collapsing of rumor, and in the challenging of community-wide support far outweigh the loss of privacy in financial matters. The sectors of society with which the university is financially allied can readily be seen and discussion of the publics with which it should be allied can take place more responsibly.

Similarly, innovations that will have effects throughout an entire institution should be discussed by the whole community. Often new channels for discussion have to be created, but the dividends in heightened morale are enormous. My own experience at Wesleyan University is as illustrative as Wertz's at MIT. During the Study of Educational Policies and Programs, which resulted in a number of major innovations, every conceivable device was used to promote discussion: open hearings, trustee-faculty conferences, faculty-consultant discussions, all-school meetings, student forums, and so forth. Several observers have related the success of the study in large measure to the achievement of genuine community-wide discussion.

When one considers that within a single complex campus it may take years for so modest, though important, a matter as a change in teaching methods in one department to become known in other departments, the enormity of the challenge is clear. But without communication circulation is inhibited. And without circulation there can be little genuine change.

Strategies for change must take into account the attitudes of those within the university. Although the dramatic model is the most appropriate for understanding the development of an academic institution, nevertheless the majority of those within the institution generally understand its development like the growth of a stalagmite: drop on drop slowly becoming a particular configuration. Therefore, proponents of academic change should heed our first strategic axiom: Stress the ways in which the new program being advocated is not totally discontinuous with the past but is a natural transformation of it—a modulation from past forms to new forms newly appropriate. Stress the ways in which the new forms naturally relate to already existing ones. The sense of connectedness expedites change. Radical discontinuity is anathema in academia.

In the exhibition of continuity within bold departures, the distinctions between the institution's ultimate goals (or commitments), its structural forms (or programs), and its specific functions (or policies) are important. Wherever possible, wise advocates of academic reform will argue that the changes in forms or functions being proposed do not alter the institution's ultimate goals (for example, "the education of youth in reference to the public good"[17]) but actually contribute to the realization of those goals in the present circumstances and for the immediate future. Even if the aim is an alteration in the institution's fundamental goals, it is best approached through changes in programs and policies, with the insistence that these changes grow naturally and organically out of previous patterns, and that these new forms and functions in turn illumine a new purpose or mission for the university. The development of the social inquiry program at MIT proceeded on this

[17] *The Catalogue,* Wesleyan University. Wesleyan's President Etherington has repeatedly insisted that there is no Wesleyan in settled form or function. There is simply a Wesleyan in commitment to the education of youth in reference to the public good, however that reference may lead the institution from time to time.

strategy. Wertz writes: "The operative assumption was that a new curriculum should maintain continuity with related existent studies and add to them, rather than seek to transform the old curriculum suddenly and provocatively."

The sense of connectedness is related to the fact that academic institutions generally change by accretion, simply adding new functions to existing ones. The process of the initiation, growth, and eventual encompassing of new programs or policies—the plateaus of formalization—is a familiar one. Both Hefferlin and Hodgkinson clearly describe the process. Hefferlin says:

The process may involve only one person: a declining major like Greek finally disappears when the classics professor retires. Or a new professor brings from graduate school an interest in solar spectroscopy. He attracts research support and assistants; he eventually may teach one or two courses in the subject; he may win the appointment of a similarly-minded colleague to the faculty; and if he moves on or retires, the central administration may find that a successor is expected to be appointed to continue the program: the field has become institutionalized.[18]

Hodgkinson is equally illuminating:

An institution probably would not set up a department of psycholinguistics with one swift stroke. A more likely series of events, occurring over a matter of years, would be: a change in the wording of a course description would emphasize the course's psycholinguistic aspect; the course would be retitled; a research assistant might begin to do some supervised work in the area because he was "interested" in it; a faculty member might take some advisees in psycholinguistics, after which his appointment listing in the catalogue might be changed to emphasize his work in psycholinguistics; a second part-time research assistant would be added; etc. Perhaps five years after the first changing of the wording in the course description the dean or department chairman would be presented with a re-

[18] *Op. cit.*, p. 25.

quest for a new department of psycholinguistics—which is already in existence in every sense except the name.[19]

In the light of this change process, our second strategic axiom is: Even though the ultimate goal may be the transformation of an entire institution, build one step or unit at a time, taking care to secure each gain before seeking the next. Again the MIT story is instructive. The strategy, Wertz reports, "was to adopt a soft tactic that would let a program of study grow up in the existing crevices. To ask immediately for a department or major would raise administrative and political problems before the intellectual problems were sorted out. It would be better to introduce a few new courses and to draw more students into noncurricular interests in order to broaden the community of concern."

This foot in the door, one step at a time procedure seems the most effective strategy to pursue, not only out of political considerations, but because of the nature of academic institutions themselves. Like the fabled web of culture, significantly pulling one point—a program or policy—to a new position will alter the pattern and shape of the whole. In informal discussions, Hodgkinson has likened the university to a complex system of hydraulic pipes in which a new input of pressure at one point or several will result in the lid's flying off at one or several other, generally unpredictable, points in the system. Unexpected developments invariably accompany change. A number of colleges, for example, have fundamentally altered their curricula only to discover that they must radically revise their programs of academic guidance to support the new programs. Or a new organizational framework in one division of the university may be presumed to be necessary only in that division, but because of its success—greater efficiency, increased productivity, heightened morale—it is soon adopted by other divisions. After each innovation a new balance has to be established. The consequences of consequences have to be taken into account.

Because of the premium placed on connectedness and the disposition of the university to grow by accretion, the "mini-max"

[19] Hodgkinson, *loc. cit.*, p. 5.

model frequently employed elsewhere in effecting change through bargaining and negotiation is peculiarly ill-suited to the academic setting. In the mini-max model, partisans purposely overstate their goals, asking for the whole at the outset, then settling for a part closer to their genuine expectations. They over-demand, over-insist, overstate, and then fall back to a more acceptable position which is nevertheless an advance from the point from which they started.

The situation is further exacerbated when purposely overstated demands are declared nonnegotiable. Although they hope that mini-max will ensue, the nonnegotiable demand makers make that process very difficult and provide recalcitrant authorities who wish to yield on nothing an excellent excuse for conducting no negotiations. They suddenly become literalists in a game being played in the dialect of hyperbole. Purposely inflated demands are difficult enough to handle and often become completely self-defeating when labelled nonnegotiable.

The MIT story clearly illustrates that if there is to be a mini-max situation, it is far better that it be circumstantial rather than calculated or programmed. As Wertz wrote in a personal communication:

Social Inquiry feels in the closing months of the Spring Term of 1969 that its "time" may be at hand, much earlier than expected. The various unexpected events of the year, especially the "March 4th movement," have been escalating confrontation politics in recent weeks. Students are now including in their demands the establishment of a social inquiry program; the administration may find it more rational to adopt social inquiry than to break Department of Defense contracts.

Instead of a calculated mini-max procedure, the generally less used "stone-on-stone" model seems better suited for achieving academic reform: Say what is meant clearly; declare what is demanded carefully; mean what is said. The natural skepticism of initially cautious colleagues is dissipated as each step of a new venture proves itself. With their suspicions allayed they are more inclined to support—or at least cease to block—the proposed change.

The key to making this model work, however, is a commitment by the ultimate decision-making body—whether trustees, administration, or academic senate—to render a decision by a specified date. Failure to do so fuels the fires of proponents of reform who contend that they are getting the runaround. Orderly change thus depends in great measure on establishing and meeting announced deadlines for decision and not letting deliberations wear on endlessly.

Our third strategic axiom follows from the first two: In a variety of ways, internal self-discipline must be exercised by the group seeking innovation. Rarely is a single goal sought in any proposed academic reform. Rather several aims are usually sought simultaneously. As the advocate group grows in size—as it has to for the reform to be instituted—it is very important that all its members agree about how they rank their various aims. The group must scale its goals from most important to least, agreeing to postpone or give up some of the least important for the sake of those with the highest priority. A shared understanding of what is most important is crucial. At MIT, for example, some wanted to move within the first year to a completely radicalized curriculum (pass-no pass grading, student-run courses, and so forth) while the majority insisted on a more deliberate approach and consciously scaled their priorities.

The reform group must be willing to work on several fronts simultaneously with a keen sense of the long as well as the short term. If the president, for example, needs widening of his openness to advocacy, group members must encourage his openness to new opinions even when the positions being urged are not their own special concerns. For the long run it is very much to their advantage if he grows in his ability to entertain advocacy. Again, if the number of hurdles required for the passing of any proposal is formidable and the procedures for passage unwieldy, then advocates of reform will work for a reduction in the number of those hurdles even when their own proposals are not under consideration. All efforts at positive change benefit by the streamlining of procedures.

Group members will also work for the creation of alternative routes for gaining approval so that, if one channel is blocked, there are others open. In short, advocates of change in the university must nurture in themselves a long-range sense of the whole which is reflected in indirect as well as direct efforts on behalf of academic reform. They must develop a sense of the whole beyond their group self-interest, a sense that requires taking the state of the world into account. And they must cultivate patience, that most difficult of qualities for those possessed of the sense of urgency for change.

Frequently the elements of reform are not present as long as considerations are limited to individuals or constituencies within the campus itself. When this fact is placed in the context of our general principles the fourth strategic axiom emerges: Enlist and cultivate those marginal members of the university who are inclined to positive change. Hefferlin characterizes a marginal member as "anyone associated with the institution whose livelihood is not dependent on it. If a person is psychologically or financially dependent on his membership in the institution, he is not marginal to it but is instead an insider. Typical marginal members of colleges and universities are trustees, alumni, visiting lecturers, patrons, and consultants. Without the influence of such marginal members most academic institutions will have difficulty in maintaining continuous reform."[20]

Academic reform thus seems best assured by a continuously fluctuating system of external pressure and internal response, where decisive power is not localized continually in any one role but shifts from the members within the organization to outsiders and back again. Progressive academic change appears to depend on the influence of these borderline individuals—sometimes in the institution but not of it—who oversee and affect its operations. In a number of institutions where change is occurring with a minimum of friction and a maximum of amity, the work of marginal members is the explanation. Frequently unexpected alliances develop between radical students and change-oriented trustees who team with reformist administrators to bring along a recalcitrant faculty. Since pressure for reform is often introduced into the campus from outside

[20] *Op. cit.*, p. 159.

rather than from within, it is important to encourage those marginal members of the community who by persuasion and positioning can serve as emissaries of change.

For the sake of ongoing, amicable change, a fifth strategic axiom is crucial: Establish units devoted to research and development of the college or university itself. Such units would result in continuous change and restructuring instead of today's sporadic innovations. Watson has written on this point:

Although higher education, by research in other fields, has been responsible for immense acceleration in technology and has led most lively corporations to increase the proportion of their budget allocated to research and development, the educational institutions have devoted only negligible amounts to evaluation and improvement of their own operations. When a university begins to subsidize research and development within its own bailiwick to something like the extent that industry now supports this function, the effect on faculty will be impressive. . . . The goal of a good R and D service in a university should be the self-renewal that is a constant, cumulative flow. It should become integral.[21]

A virtually endless list of tactical suggestions for effecting academic change grows out of these principles and strategic axioms. Here it is necessary for me to speak in generalizations even when discussing tactics, the most concrete level in producing change. Tactics, however, are the reality that most needs to be shaped to fit particular, local situations—the reality that most eludes generalization. We shall therefore make only five tactical suggestions, aware that there are many more considerations to be included in such a list, but that they are better framed in a given situation to fit particular circumstances. We offer, in general terms, the following tactical counsel.

First, even though advocacy is pursued indirectly as well as directly, for the long haul as well as the short term, operate in any given moment on a manageable number of fronts. The number of points at which advocacy can be pursued is clearly a function of

[21] Watson, *loc. cit.*, pp. 4–5.

the size of the reform group and the degree of its internal differentiation. Because of a habit of mind that makes them think that they are especially trained to see the long range implications of present innovations, academicians, especially reformers, are especially prone to get ahead of themselves in the processes of change—to confuse second and third stage moves with first stage ones. The success of the MIT curricular change is in large measure related to the deliberateness with which it was pursued. Wertz says: "The steering committee had three fronts on which it struggled during the summer of 1968: bureaucratic, intellectual, and programmatic. The first of these involved getting a foot in the door, finding a minimal amount of support from the Institute. . . . Drawing up an intellectual statement outlining the need for and nature of the new program required a surprising amount of effort, but when completed it became a calling card attracting new people into the program. The third front took the most time, for we sought to have three new courses taught in the Humanities Department."

Second, avoid overextension, certainly in its most typical forms—premature demands or premature structure. There are some innovations that can be called for effectively only from the platform of some other already established ones. If urged before solid foundations are laid the entire package of innovative proposals can be imperiled. Asking for too much, we get nothing. Premature or excessive structuring of new programs is another typical form of overextension to be guarded against. Establish only those structures absolutely necessary for the functioning of the new venture.

Third, guarantee those who must approve the reform that it will be systematically monitored and provisions made for its dissolution if, within a reasonable and explicit period of time, it fails to realize its aims or eventually no longer serves its functions. Equally important is the early identification of the agency that will conduct the evaluation and the assurance of its impartiality. Martin Trow remarks that "if every new academic program had a 'destruct mechanism' built into it, academic review councils might be markedly less hesitant to approve them."[22] Certainly the specter of pro-

[22] *Op. cit.*, p. 16.

liferating programs with eternal institutional life haunts many academic decision-makers—an apprehension which the development of many universities, like the growth of post-New Deal federal bureaucracy, does nothing to allay. Rather than seeking timeless leases for their new programs, proponents of reform should seek authorization simply to operate for a reasonable period of time. From the outset evaluation procedures should be developed and the courage cultivated in the program's proponents to declare their program at an end if in fact, in the stated time, it does not measure up. There is something compelling about the honesty of academicians moved to trigger the destruct mechanism on their own beloved, but failing, projects.

Fourth, devote serious attention and substantial effort to the public interpretation of the proposed policy or program, both within and without the campus community. The suspicion that conspiracy is afoot is a frequent response of cautious members within the university to rumors of change, while the assumption that destructive radicalism will inform any change is often the response of people outside the university. Telling the true story openly is an important and indispensable way to allay these apprehensions. The whole story need not be told—nor can it always be. (Who indeed ever knows the whole story?) But the less threatening and conspiratorial a movement toward change appears, the greater the likelihood of its acceptance. Look once more at MIT: "We consciously sought to avoid tactics that would invoke the censure of the whole community. . . . We worked very hard to explain ourselves to our colleagues. . . . Careful and personal interpretation of the nature and purpose of innovation to individual faculty members made the innovation much easier."

Fifth, insofar as possible, initially seek outside funding for the new program. The development of new programs occurs most easily when new resources, specifically for these projects, are available. And acceptance of the initial diversion of existing funds to a new venture is forthcoming only when there is widespread agreement that the enterprise formerly receiving those funds is obsolete or disfunctional.

The dispassionate tone of my essay now must shift to a concluding comment of passionate urgency. The presupposition of this essay that it is still possible to reform institutions of higher education in America through reasonable processes without having to destroy them and begin afresh is increasingly being challenged. It is the recalcitrance of so many universities and their resistance to reform that are deepening the doubts about their malleability and reinforcing the revolutionary alternative.

In terms of our dramatic view of institutional history, it should be clear that this is a supreme occasion for decision by American colleges and universities. Either they will move through processes of academic reform not unlike those suggested here to break their bondage to things as they are, to recover commitment to students as their primary clientele, to conceive for themselves another mission that weds intellectual inquiry with social involvement, or they will be overtaken, disrupted, and irreparably damaged by those who have lost faith in reform. I am convinced that with imaginative leadership and cooperation among members of an academic institution it is still possible for a university to overcome the shackles of its past, resist the pressures of inertia, and truly become a new institution. There is precious little time to confirm this hypothesis. The moment of truth is now at hand.

Richard Wertz

An Experience of Curricular Change

VI

This story records the failures and successes of an attempt at curricular innovation within the social and intellectual culture of MIT. Perhaps the chronicle of action (and reaction) to obtain a new undergraduate program will yield insights to others concerned about behavior in the university or to others looking for a strategy for radical curricular change.

No social scientist has tried to describe MIT as a social organization, and most faculty and students are puzzled by how decisions are made there. In the loose organization of nearly autonomous departments and schools—engineering, science, humanities and social science, architecture, and management—the impression is widely held that anyone having a strong idea and support for it can do almost anything. This impression reflects accurately the expansive role of science and technology in our culture, for the academic budget of this technological institution increased at the rate of 15 per cent a year from 1953 to 1968. The impression also typifies the traditional value placed upon the freedom of the scientist to explore and initiate. Initiative and new enterprises are subject to review; yet the review appears to differ according to the source of the initiative and the nature of the enterprise. Government, industry, and foundations impinge upon the Institute so strongly that it has an atmosphere of growth in which it is nearly impossible to determine how the value of innovation is measured, and to establish a rigorous process of decision-making. In this atmosphere the relative powers of individuals, departments, and the administration are always obscure. So the impression of nearly boundless opportunity for innovation prevails; yet no certainty exists about how a decision to accept or limit opportunity must be made, or on what grounds innovation would be educationally substantive and socially worthwhile.

This permissive and expansive educational environment provoked the attempt to introduce a new major. As the amount of government-sponsored war research increased, students and faculty after 1965 began to complain that the intellectual integrity of the Institute was threatened; classified work, courses requiring security clearance, and the involvement of students in war work were objected to as both educationally and morally detrimental. There were teach-ins and exposures. In May of 1966 the Center for International Studies was revealed to have been receiving substantial aid from the C.I.A. The student newspaper reported that several professors had refused to pay their taxes because of the Vietnam War. Most revealing, however, was a guest editorial by the MIT Society for Social Responsibility, which wondered why an institution as deeply engaged as MIT in shaping society did not provide curricular analysis of the tremendous issues implicit in these efforts.

In the following year two professors broke the barrier of silence about these concerns; they taught a course in "Intellectuals and Social Change," which became enormously popular. More than a hundred Harvard students cross-registered for it during one term. The catalogue description indicates its scope:

The role and responsibility of individuals who challenge the assumptions of established political and social order, and who are concerned with ideas and their consequences. Discussion of current issues that have given rise to action and protest, in particular: American foreign policy, the problem of poverty, the Negro revolution, the role of university students. Questions of individual commitment, and the available alternatives for action. Historical background, with emphasis on socialist, anarchist, and liberal responses to recurrent problems which have faced the committed individual since the Enlightenment and Industrial Revolution. Study of the conditioning of these responses by the relation of intellectuals to established institutions such as government and the universities.

When I came to MIT in 1966–1967, this course was the center for students disaffected with society. In February, 1967, a teach-in drew four hundred students. In April, an antiwar week was announced. Other professors were holding open discussion of the immorality of the war. SDS at MIT published a pamphlet on "MIT and the Warfare State," a remarkable indictment of war research for impairing the intellectual and academic climate. These activities did not disrupt the outward calm of the Institute, but discussion of the war was becoming more intense, and a polarization of opinion was beginning. By the end of the school year in the spring of 1967, a community of protest existed, and it was sharing a rather carefully articulated intellectual position. Radical students had found that faculty would support them, and that faculty support was invaluable for analysis and internal politics. Henceforth, the two groups would work as one on most issues.

During the summer of 1967 Cambridge was alive with organizing activities. Resistance groups had perhaps the most enduring significance. Faculty set up a variety of support activities, especially draft counselling. When schools opened in the fall, the toughness of the protest was greater. Harvard students blocked a Dow Chemical Company recruiter. At once the MIT protest community met to plan action for Dow's visit to MIT on November 6. Students initiated this planning; but, unlike their mates at Harvard, they asked the faculty to support them. About sixty faculty members met and agreed to support the students if they conducted a non-obstructive demonstration. Faculty argued that the tactic of obstruction assumed that "evil" recruiters should not be allowed to pollute the "pure" academic community; since this distinction was patently false, the tactic could make no valid point. Moreover, obstructionist behavior would, in effect, obscure the issue being raised: that students should not misuse their skills. Why give conservatives and liberals a delightful false issue such as freedom of speech and access? Students agreed. MIT had a strong demonstration, its day in the press, and no bitter discipline disputes. The administration was proud of the students. President Howard Johnson said in reference to the demonstration: "It is a principle of the university to permit, provide, and protect an environment where dissent is possible. . . . On the other hand, it is important that such protest not become abusive or limit the reasonable rights of others."[1] The community of concern—both students and faculty—had begun to take action. In a letter to the student newspaper, the president of Students for a Democratic Society declined to take credit for the event, saying his organization was amazed by the number who came forward to take part.

In all the activity during the protean school year of 1967–1968, what became distinctive about MIT's community of protest was the desire for intellectual clarity and perspective on social problems and for protest action which highlighted concrete issues. The community succeeded in avoiding confusing tactics and violent actions. In addition, the administration appeared sympathetic to responsible student protest, and many faculty were willing to spend time planning and talking with students about issues and actions. It was in this tolerant atmosphere that some students conceived the idea of enlarging the course "Intellectuals and Social Change" into an undergraduate program that would be concerned with the role of intellectuals and of the technical intelligentsia in social problems.

[1] H. Johnson, *The Technologist,* 1967, *87*(42), 1.

The idea was attractive. The number of faculty supporting an interdisciplinary program was clearly impressive, and the level of student interest high. A group of faculty and students met in May, 1968, to map out strategy and tactics for a broader program.

The meeting discussed both what was desirable and what was possible in a new curricular program. What was desirable was consideration of serious social problems and the role of intellectuals in them in a manner different from traditional social science methods, a program that provided for the organic growth of critical intellectual concerns unencumbered by extrinsic policy pressures, a program in which students could play an active role in shaping the curricula. What was possible was not yet clear, but the meeting was optimistic about administrative support. The conclusion was to adopt a soft tactic that would let a program of study grow up in the existing crevices. To ask immediately for a department or major would raise administrative and political problems before the intellectual problems were sorted out. It would be better to introduce a few new courses and to draw more students into noncurricular interests in order to broaden the community of concern and learn its interests. The operative assumption was that a new curriculum should maintain continuity with related existent studies and add to them, rather than seek to transform the old curriculum suddenly and provocatively. A steering committee was appointed to work during the summer drawing up a statement of intent and organizing for the fall. It was composed of students and faculty.

The steering committee had three fronts on which it struggled during the summer of 1968: bureaucratic, intellectual, and programmatic. The first of these involved getting a foot in the door, finding a minimal amount of support from the Institute. We asked for and received a part-time secretary, an office, mailing privileges, reproducing privileges, and one-third time off for a faculty coordinator. Drawing up an intellectual statement outlining the need for and the nature of the new program required a surprising amount of effort, but when completed became a calling card attracting new people into the program. The third front took the most time, for we sought to have three new courses taught in the Humanities Department and it is difficult to obtain approval in the summer.

Three new courses were given for credit in the fall of 1968. I will not digress to describe the pain and the pleasure they created. Each course was requested by a different group of students. Students in a regularly offered course, "Russian and American Diplomacy," asked for a new course that would explore revisionist views of the cold war and enable them to research them. This request seemed fitting at MIT where political science has stressed cold war ideology. The course, taught by a member of the history faculty, produced some impressive student papers. A second group of students, engaged in a local tutoring program funded by the Office of Equal Opportunity and MIT asked for a yearlong seminar on problems of urban education. A professor of literature, a specialist in urban linguistics and education, agreed to teach it; he sought out parents of tutees to be members of the seminar and focused the seminar on assessment of educational needs in MIT's particular neighborhood.

These two courses were creative and fruitful; they are models of curricular innovation that meets student interest and results in concrete educational relevance. The third course, however, illustrates the problems of some student initiative. A group of students who had been active in political protest asked for a student-directed course on "Responsibility," and they found a professor of philosophy to sponsor it. After the first class meeting the course gained notoriety by petitioning the Committee on Educational Policy for a pass-pass grading system; that is, they asked that a student be assured of passing a course merely by registering for it. This system would, they argued, remove the onerous pressures for certification, for winning the instructor's approval; it would dignify students and encourage them to be responsible. The petition created a minor storm on the faculty committee.

The sponsoring professor and the steering committee were embarrassed by this development, but a lesson about experiments in student-conducted courses was learned. At that time, many radical students' creativity seemed to be in making administrative suggestions for educational reform that would diminish authority, which they found oppressive. At MIT, which retains a required core curriculum in mathematics, physics, chemistry, and humanities, and rigorous departmental requirements, resistance to notions of requirements, disciplines, and propaedeutic sequences is an understandably humane concern, but a concern not furthered by demands to abolish grades and professors at once. But then the time scales of faculty and students differ markedly.

What the steering committee learned from these experiments has been applied in sponsoring new courses in subsequent semesters. In the spring term of 1969, students asked for a course on anarchism. They said they knew nothing about the literature of anarchism, its place in the history of philosophy and society, or what it might imply for current social alternatives; they willingly agreed that a professor should draw up a preliminary reading list, which they would follow until they could generate questions of their own. In this case, the professor's authority consisted of being more knowledgeable; students' curiosity in turn was respected. The steering committee was happy to sponsor this genuinely educational request. In subsequent terms, a number of other courses were taught by faculty responding to student interest, following the same model.

By the end of the summer of 1968 the committee had won a bureaucratic foothold, written a statement of intent, and launched a few courses. The next step in our strategy consisted of initiating noncurricular seminars for faculty and students to discuss social questions especially relevant to MIT. We hoped these seminars would enlarge the community of concern and produce educational ideas that could become subjects for curricula. When we asked the administration to circulate invitations to these noncurricular seminars, we were asked to obtain the approval of the Committee on Educational Policy. At a special, hastily called meeting, the CEP expressed general approval (how could they disapprove inquiry about social problems?) but issued several warnings. They thought nothing seriously educational could be noncurricular, for only "experts" were equipped to speak knowledgeably on these questions. They also warned us against allowing the inquiry to focus on MIT as a scene of social problems: it would be better to look at society at large.

More than three hundred people attended the organizational meeting; they split into smaller groups on specific problems and continued to meet weekly. People came and went, but the group met throughout most of the term. Their topics were MIT and the community, science and society, educational innovation, communal living, and student-faculty relations. The groups got to the Institute's sore spots almost at once. Faculty attendance was high in some groups; where the faculty continued to attend, the vitality of the groups was high. The unavoidable fatigue factor in MIT extracurricular life eventually depressed the groups, and, in the long run, they did not produce any solid educational suggestions. But they provided an opportunity to discuss issues informally, and to have a different perspective on the educational and scientific environment. Some students, active in social inquiry, were also active in the war protest that in 1968 took the form of harboring absentee soldiers.

We have often jokingly said that MIT's sanctuary of an AWOL soldier was our best social and educational event. MIT was galvanized as never before by this protest. When hundreds of students were sleeping in the student center, thousands were visiting it each day, the best entertainers were donating their time, and the national press was covering it, an atmosphere of incredible intensity and festivity took over. The articulate soldier, the continuous open debate on tactics and politics, the negotiation with other student groups who had to cancel scheduled activities, the negotiations with the administration, the mixing of professional radicals, motorcycle clubbers, professors, horrified conservatives, and technologically skilled security freaks blew the lid off. The value of this extrastructural community happening was that everyone involved learned something about his university and himself that would bear fruit in later months.

After an exhausting week of togetherness the student organizers decided that their health and the advancement of the cause demanded an end of the public affair. The arresting officers were obviously in no hurry to try to take a soldier from a crowd of six hundred or one thousand people, no matter how nonviolent they intended to be. The students asked the administration if the soldier could attend classes, sleep in dormitories, and "become human." But this request coincided with the right-wing reaction, which had taken a week to gather weight around the country and at the school.

The administration had expressed privately its sympathy with the protest activity, allowing the resistance to use student space. But it had to resist publicly the spread of sanctuary into official space. Rumors spread of discipline against faculty persons who might invite the soldier to class. Liberal faculty, many of whom had not been deeply involved in sanctuary, were aroused by this seeming restriction on their freedom. Radical faculty pleaded with both administration and liberals to avoid a quarrel over a non-issue. The students remained calm, for their aim was to protest not for academic freedom but against the war, and they were not going to be drawn into a needless quarrel. They withdrew their request and announced the end of the sanctuary in its public form. A lesson was clear in this: the MIT administration could be a powerful ally and protector, but it was easily embarrassed by the overexposure entailed by public quarrels and demonstrations. In these instances it had to conform to the dominant opinion of the whole community, a largely conservative view that values the status quo. Curricular change, therefore, should avoid tactics that would invoke the censure of the larger community.

By November, 1968, the steering committee agreed to discuss a major in social inquiry. Catalogue copy was due by March and the committee foresaw, correctly, months of deliberation about any proposal. A working copy was drawn up and mailed to several hundred people for their comments. By December a final draft was completed and submitted to the policy committee of the Humanities Department. The Humanities Department, composed of the four sections of music, literature, philosophy, and history, is one of five departments in the School of Humanities and Social Science, which embraces also economics, political science, psychology, and language and linguistics. The policy committee is composed of the heads of the four sections and the chairman. It would have to approve any new major.

The reaction of the policy committee was ambivalent. Most members believed that the importance of such an intellectual-educational concern was clear; however, there were serious reasons why it should not have a place in this department. One member said that if Humanities adopted this major, it would absolve all other departments from consideration of social responsibility. Another argued that a "social inquirer" had no professional stance, would not command intellectual respectability within the Institute, and would stir up trouble for the department within the Institute by appearing to be ideological. But enough members thought these reasons either untrue or insubstantial enough to halt committee discussion. The committee called a meeting of all faculty and staff of the department to discuss the proposal.

By the time of the meeting, forty members of the department had signed a petition asking the policy committee to accept the proposal for a new major. Careful and personal interpretation of the nature and purpose of innovation to individual faculty members made the program clearer and more acceptable. When younger faculty spoke to older ones, many of the latter would not sign the petition, but agreed not to oppose it either. Without personal discussion, a proposal for change would have been even more misunderstood, however clearly articulated, because faculty do not usually read such things carefully and generally feel threatened by change. In the meeting, the administrative shape of the major was clarified; the faculty present voted unanimously for the program. However, many faculty were not present of course.

The steering committee was buoyed by the vote, however, and quickly drew up a catalogue description of the major and requested approval of two new yearlong seminars. But the policy committee at its next meeting felt that no decision had been made. Moreover, the committee doubted whether the "inquirers" had the competence to set up such a major, whether the major had indeed any intellectual respectability, and whether any students wanted to take it. The dean of the School of Humanities and Social Science was present at this meeting; he suggested an informal meeting with the other faculties of the school to discuss the proposal, because if the major were sent to the Committee on Educational Policy, this committee would want to know what other departments in the school thought of the major, since it was interdisciplinary.

The dean's decision could be viewed as a cynical delaying tactic or as a genuine desire to air opinions. At any rate, the steering committee carefully spelled out a rationale and program for the major, for so the academic game is played. For two hours a member of the steering committee presented the rationale to the school's faculties, emphasizing how the fact-value problem in the American academy limited the scope and sometimes the quality of scholarship. He pointed to lack of scholarship about the anarchists in the Spanish Civil War, the growth of revisionist views of the cold war outside the academy, and so forth. Perhaps the fact-value problem could not be solved, but some means was needed to increase awareness of its limiting action in professionalized study, and some consideration was needed of the shapes ideology took in an industrialized society and how the ideology affected study and action in regard to social issues.

Reactions to the proposal took many forms. The more responsible reactions questioned whether the proposal could do what we hoped to do, asked what academic standards could be applied to judge such a program, or concerned the administration of the program. After drinks and dinner the discussion continued. There was a mood of good feeling, in part, perhaps, because the faculties of the school had not met in a decade. Altogether the meeting brought a net gain. Misconceptions were removed; a clearer impression of the openness of the program to participation by others was created; a common sense of the failure of the departments to study ideologies and social problems was acknowledged; several younger faculty put the program on their personal agendas.

We never expected this meeting to endorse the program. In fact, we had decided prior to the meeting to withdraw the request for a major at that time, and to ask only for the introduction of several new courses. We needed to demonstrate the quality of and desire for these courses and to enlist more faculty and students in the program. Having tested the political strength of our support and having found it not sufficient to overcome nervousness and misunderstanding, we elected to follow the path of quiet pressure, knowing that in the academy an accomplished fact is always more readily accepted than a totally new program.

Specifically, we proposed in the fall of 1969 an experimental, four-year program in which any student might minor, with courses for credit taught by regular, part-time, or temporary faculty. This proposal was accepted, although academic finances have radically altered, making new programs less viable, and the public image of radicalism has become, if anything, more repellent than before.

The persistent pressure we have exerted for curricular change has revealed some misjudgment and confusion in our strategy and aims. Although we have always known that we were considered a radical group, that is, antiwar, skeptical, unusually conversant with many student organizations, well-organized, we did not do everything we could to remove this label. In fact, we were not all radicals. But whatever our real diversity, we have appeared to be radicals at MIT. If our only aim had been to secure a new major, we should have more quickly extended our interpretive function to sympathetic faculty in other departments of the School of Humanities and Social Science, thereby strengthening our base of power, and diluting the radical coloration of our group. The potential danger of that strategy was that our program would become merely another interdepartmental, interdisciplinary major; a coherent perspective on social problems would be sacrificed to quick change.

By operating on many fronts at one time, we gave the impression that the social inquiry program had nearly limitless aims. Radical students were always shifting their ground: sanctuary, student government reform, grading reform, student-initiated subjects, alteration of the standards, sharing of faculty power were demanded at various times; many of us were drawn into these activities as consultants or advocates. And the students who wanted change of any kind were drawn to the one semiofficial organization that promised innovation. It was genuinely difficult for our critics to discern what we meant by social inquiry. Making our aim clear by using what I have called the interpretive function was always consciously important to us (we early disavowed the pass-pass proposal), but our critics were quick to think we shared some "crazy" student aim. This is known as the escalation of guilt, or being the scapegoat. It requires patient interpretation.

The most serious paradox of curricular innovation, especially if it is consonant with the spirit of much student thinking, lies in the specification of goals. The rule seems to be that the more specific the goal is, the less the enthusiasm will be. Being a community in which student enthusiasm and delight had a place meant much to us; this delight often issued in student protests which grew out of a sense of the dehumanizing nature of many rules and requirements. However, one cannot easily translate a mood into a major, for the latter requires precise specification in order to gain approval and to have intellectual substantiality. The paradox is not revealed by a neat split between faculty and students. Some faculty believed the radical spirit to be more important than the development of a radical curriculum. Some students wanted an intellectually satisfying explanation of their society's predicament more than they wanted the ebb and flow of affective action. Surely it is necessary to make a place for both affective and cognitive elements in a community of concern. At present the affective elements aim at definition and excitement through action rather than through intellectual search, but I believe the two elements can abide together and that, at MIT, they will come together, as long as we are not under the obligation of specifying for at least another year concrete subjects, sequences, and requirements associated with a major. Substantial intellectual work can occur outside a major. A community can exist without having an official place within a university. The essential goal is developing a community within which an integration of affective and cognitive styles can occur.

Pressure for curricular change, by definition, involves calling to account the social myth of an educational institution. It reveals the dilemmas, commitments, and assumptions within a social myth, for pressure for change, even when observing the proprieties of academic discourse, profoundly threatens social roles, traditions, and symbols. Like student protests, it serves notice that the social myth is not the reality perceived or sought.

What has our experience taught us about our social myth? At the basis of the university's self-understanding lies the assumption of its purity. Dedicated to service, like the churches, it is free of the profit motive of business, and, unlike the churches, free from indoctrination. It is free from the corruption and coercion of political institutions. The myth of purity has grown in historical association with the other dominant institutions of society. The myth stresses that the academy is free internally for unlimited, innocent exchange of ideas, and externally for service. The free, open marketplace of ideas seeks no profit and employs no coercion in the search for truth. Notions of sanity, civility, self-sacrifice, and self-emptying, religiously inspired, inform this myth. It would be ridiculous to be cynically supercilious toward the myth, for radicals share its assumptions too; most radical critique believes, however, that purity lies in the future rather than the past or present. The problem, of course, is to take the transformed present into the future. Curricular reform that aims at understanding the present, its structure and tendencies, is an intellectual prerequisite for that venture.

Edward Schwartz

The New University

VII

Is it possible to build a new university? How might this task be accomplished? These questions lie at the core of this volume. In asking the questions we assume several notions—that the social movements of the sixties have heightened public, particularly youth, consciousness of standards of humanness which were not considered as important in previous years; that our universities have failed, so far, to meet these standards; and that serious institutional change will be necessary for the university to revitalize itself. We have tried to determine what the new standards are; what the university is in relation to them; and how the necessary change may best be achieved. Further, we are concerned with the impact which educational change might have on social and political change.

The way we have gone about this task has been a source of considerable frustration to me. Apart from my long-standing disquiet in extended meetings with liberals, I have often felt that the conversation has led nowhere. Perhaps I have been unfair; my background is in politics and sociology, not theology. Certain of the lengthy excursions into theological questions have been unintelligible to me. Yet I could not help thinking at several points that our endless discussions of existential consciousness, Norman O. Brown, teleological man, and the wondrous diversity of higher education have had nothing to do with the dialogues which currently animate the movements for educational change within the National Student Association and the movements for social and political change within Students for a Democratic Society.

The formal contours of our discussions have not been satisfying either. On the one hand, we have Hodgkinson's Walden U. —a delightful place, to be sure, and well worth starting, but serving primarily to test a new process by which the traditional enterprise of the university, intellectual inquiry, might be better fulfilled. On the other hand, we confront Maguire's pleas for discussions of strategy, realized in Wertz's account of the battle for social inquiry at MIT. One wonders, however, what relationship exists between building the department at MIT and building a new kind of MIT. My repeated questions on this score remain unanswered, which suggests to me why radical students at MIT might feel frustrated at the way the department is being developed.

Two descriptive commentaries have been offered. Callahan has presented us with a cogent discussion of the fact-value problem in university epistemology; I cannot help feeling that this is nice but insufficient. To consider the university crisis, we must deal with a few specific facts of the university and weigh them against certain values of our own, rather than confine ourselves to an attack on higher education for confusing the two areas in general. Howard's eloquent collage of the new vision limits itself in a similar fashion. In describing the joy which accompanies the cultural life of the new visionaries, he ignores the enormous political and personal strains which exist between them and the rest of America.

Then there is Shoben's chapter, the only one to grapple with both what the university is and what it might be. With my strong bias toward Saul Alinsky, however, I think that humaneness and the examined life will serve us poorly in battles against the enemies of progressive change in this country—a point made theoretically and in practice by SDS. I suspect that even the encouragement of civil liberty, the development of student participation, the admission of minority students, the creation of experiential programs, and the improvement of dormitory conditions will be insufficient to create the transformation of our universities which we seek.

To me, the seminar has mirrored, rather than transcended, the inability of liberalism to answer coherently the questions radicals are asking and the demands we make. Liberal utopians can offer no strategies to realize their utopia in the old order, except for certain pluralists who suggest we start new institutions. Liberal strategists provide no utopian vision (Maguire fought hard to bring the discussion off that level), and yell at the new left for sneering at what we believe to be inadequate proposals for change. Fellow radicals like Howard want to describe the new vision to liberals without mentioning its essential conflict with the surrounding society; sympathetic liberals like Shoben want to present the university environment to radicals in such a way as to convince us that the changes we seek can be realized within it.

My experience as a change agent in universities has made me impatient with all these approaches. The liberal vision, I have come to realize, is inadequate to what the social order, and the university, can do. Strategies liberals advocate make sense only in relation to liberal objectives. Torn by the desire to achieve change while remaining orderly, the liberal can never decide what his real priorities are. Too often, he falls back on order and demands that others do likewise. The new visionaries, however, are demanding a measure of institutional change which cannot be sponged up in this manner. Further, as joyful as we may be at parties, we are something quite different when we go into battle. Fundamentally, that is what liberals neither accept nor understand about us. We see ourselves in battle.

I want to discuss the kind of university many of us are trying to build. I want to relate our conception of what a university should be and do to what we think today's university is and does. Finally, I want to outline a few of the tactical steps and strategies we are exploring in our efforts to move the university in a different direction. We have not answered for ourselves all the questions we are asking. I merely wish to describe the framework of our debate.

First, who are we? We are young men and women who seek legitimation for the passionate life. This is not Thoreau's life of quiet contemplation in the woods, away from the multitudes, nor is it the life of the salons of eighteenth-century France so revered by the liberals. It is a life of movement and intensity, of conflict, of dialectic, of spontaneity. The passionate life is a heady flight of ecstasy, a McCluhanist square dance, a loving spoonful. It is, indeed, the new vision of Howard's essay—a vision which values the bold over the bland, the creative over the analytical, the subjective over the objective, the transformation of interpersonal reality rather than the dilution of it.

Yet it is something else as well, something which Howard does not mention. We do not write a book which discusses the identity crisis of higher education because a few of our comrades report to us that the top of the mountain looks somewhat different than John Locke imagined it to be. We write because the new visionaries have determined that they will free space in our institutions for the passionate life by any means necessary. The qualities which enable love, joy, intimacy, ecstasy, and excitement are those which also become abrasive at cruelty, explosive at repression. Consequently, the passionate life involves a certain kind of toughness—the kind of toughness needed to tell a professor or a dean that he is screwing up your life; the kind of toughness needed to face the conflicts of working in a ghetto; the kind required to march on the Pentagon, or to work nineteen hours a day to topple the United States; the kind of toughness needed to resist the draft. The new visionary is loving to those who love, cruel to those who do not, who build environments which make love impossible.

What is the nature of the university we are trying to build? What is its central principle? The new university is a community devoted to building cultural pluralism. The community constantly seeks to expand the relationships between its members, but it views the different life styles, cultural norms, and modes of expression of its citizens as enriching to the whole, rather than threatening to it.

Indeed, the commitment to cultural pluralism allows transcendence of traditional American pluralism which was built on respect for people's economic rights. Building cultural pluralism demands that the community commit economic resources to its development; that each member of the community seek to elicit and give as much of his own richness and the richness of others as he can; that the community place itself in opposition to those institutions whose operation makes cultural pluralism impossible. The participant in such a community would not simply tolerate uniqueness in men, he would revel in it, seek it, value it, want to help it. He would not simply tolerate disorder; he would demand disorder, conflict, dialectic, emotional tension, believing they are basic to the learning and being processes.

This kind of community begins, often, as a conversation between two people. The conversation expands to become an implicit learning contract between the two parties—a contract which expresses mutual commitment to take risks with one another, to share questions and resources for answering them, to trade skills. As the conversation intensifies, it draws new participants. Some cling to the original group, others spin off into their own subgroups, then return. The experimental college in San Francisco State began in this manner; it built from two people to fifteen hundred.

What of inquiry in the new university? Is it anti-intellectual? Do its members read? Participants in the new university are voracious readers. If they are guilty of any sin, it is the sin of trying to read too much simultaneously. Trying to construct a new kind of community, a new cultural pluralism, they utilize segments of every field, every discipline, every area of inquiry. The builders of the new university may on one day read a novel which clarifies some aspect of human experience, on the next a social theorist whose work facilitates consideration of alternative institutional forms, then a sociologist whose research illuminates the nature of contemporary society, and then a scientist whose technological instruments will free men to pursue humane goals.

This process varies from community to community, of course. Moreover, the participants of the new university may spend long hours in private reading, with the detachment of the most detached scientist. But when they subject themselves to the scientific discipline of detached observation, it is a temporary surrender made necessary by the task at hand, not the total surrender demanded by those who believe that the detached, orderly way of living is prerequisite to scholarship. The cultivation of the discipline useful for the absorption of certain kinds of information, or for the development of certain mental skills, often is as difficult for participants in the new university as is the cultivation of feeling and subjectivity in members of the old university. Many of the most talented members of the new university have emerged from the most exacting of the old disciplines. They are the ones who insist that learning must resist linear patterns, disciplines, formalized requirements, and patterns of classroom lectures, except when absolutely necessary to master a particular skill.

Participants in the new university major, essentially, in the process of building the new university. As each person contributes to the construction of the community, he realizes his own skills and interests, as does any developing human being, and concentrates on developing them. It is rare, however, for people in experimental colleges, for example, to be confined to one discipline.

In the new university everyone teaches and everyone learns. Authority is based on competence and it shifts to different members of the group as different needs are met. The teacher one day may be a scientist who has been asked to explain the new media; the next he may be a social scientist who has offered to explain Rousseau. Decisions affecting community life in the new university are made by the members of the community. Inasmuch as the community seeks to build cultural pluralism, wide latitude for private forms of expression is offered and encouraged.

There are no grades in the new university, but there is mutual evaluation. Evaluation is not a competitive process. One makes a commitment to another to help him grow, and that always means a commitment to mutual criticism and praise.

The members of the new university are loyal first to themselves, not to an institution. They are loyal to all who are committed to building a new pluralism or preserving what cultural pluralism remains in this country. They are loyal to those for whom private economic gain is no longer the ultimate goal. They are loyal to those who consider suppression of feelings a problem, not a necessity.

The citizen of the new university is loyal to black people and responds to the cry for black power, which he understands to be the last attempt to restore cultural pluralism to the country. He is loyal to the Vietnamese peasants whose distinctive ways have won them the epithet *gook,* the mortar shells of our armies, the opprobrium of those who call themselves defenders of a free world. He is loyal to the Indian against the Spaniard, the Irish and Italian against the Yankee, the Jew against the Christian, to all who have been persecuted in our culture, or who have been told that the price of food is the sacrifice of self to get a job.

The loyalty of people in the new university entails building the university in a manner which deemphasizes repression, privatism, and cultural exploitation on the part of participating students. It entails a commitment to seek the transformation of all institutions outside the university which reinforce the surrounding culture's dominant ideologies and politics. It entails a commitment to devote the resources of the university to an analysis of the repressive social forces, the cultural roots and underpinnings, the ideological justifications, the institutional forms, and the political tools of the surrounding society. It entails a commitment to consider alternative models for the new society, alternative theories for the new vision of man, alternative views of the new loyalty, and alternative strategies for achieving these goals.

The new university legitimates direct action in the community. Action teaches, as does thought. Learning is being is acting is learning. A serious community action group in a ghetto, committed to both the change and the examination of the internal process of the action group, is certainly part of the new university, as are the few serious learning-living-acting communes around the country. The new university does not freeze learning into boxes called classroom and professor. Life is learning; learning is life.

The new university is passionate people seeking community, building cultural pluralism, reading and absorbing the surrounding world, sharing skills and talents with one another, criticizing or praising work as it deserves one or the other, teaching and being taught by everyone in the group, developing loyalties to all those whom the creation of cultural pluralism will serve, and developing the skills with which society may realize the new vision.

The new university differs from Hodgkinson's Walden U. In Walden U., the community is structured to increase possibilities for inquiry; in the new university, possibilities for inquiry are provided so that the student-teachers may enrich the life of the community. One attends the new university not simply to inquire, but to share in the community, to build, and to teach, in the broadest, most demanding sense.

The differences between the new university and the present one should be apparent. Yet it will be useful to review the characteristics of the present university, in order to emphasize the frustration which the new visionaries face in trying to change it.

The present university's ideal man is Gene in *A Separate Peace*[1]—that competent analyst of today's world, tolerant of mild deviation from the norm, skilled in the techniques of scientific investigation, contemplative in spirit and in style, moderately liberal in politics, blessed with a balanced temper in argument, committed to rational persuasion, and fully prepared to assume a high position in one of the new industrial state's finest corporations or in one of its government agencies.

The present university's ideal man is the McCarthy worker who easily shifts to Humphrey as the lesser of two evils. He is the student government representative who sees the need for a black studies department but not the need to take over a building to get it; whose periodic disagreements with the university president do not interfere with a genuine respect for the man and a concern for his problems; whose course load includes a few guts, a few grinds. His life includes a few laughs, a few furrowed brows, but no tears because a man is not supposed to cry. He is stronger than J. Alfred Prufrock, more sensitive than Babbitt, at peace in a way that Richard Corey must never have been.

The central principle of the present university can be seen

[1] J. Knowles, *A Separate Peace* (New York: Macmillan, 1960).

in the requirements it places on its students. The requirements are no longer primarily related to subject matter or to knowledge. They remain, however, wedded to a process which breaks time and space into easily digestible units. The commitment a student makes to the university is that he will accumulate a certain number of credit hours, divided into specified subject units, each of which is controlled by a given professor. The total of all this, particularly if balanced with a concentration of several units in one area, is called an education.

The university does not care how the student breaks his hours up, as long as he has enough in his area and enough to graduate. The institution is not terribly concerned with what the student does within these units, although a few professors whom the student encounters along the way may care. Moreover, neither institution nor professor is terribly concerned about what happens to students outside those special blocks of time, unless the student intrudes upon somebody else's block of time or on the administration's block of time or interferes with his own ability to meet the university's demands.

To the extent that the university exacts a commitment beyond that just outlined, it is a commitment to cultivate the rational style, to repress passions which contribute to disorder, to cultivate detachment from events and a prudent distance between people, to value accommodation and compromise in all social and political situations, regardless of who is involved, and to respect standards of common courtesy to all men.

Even if these values were not also encouraged outside the classroom, the academic process, which teaches people that learning and life can be blocked off into bite-size units of time, would be sufficient to cultivate these presumed virtues. He who can develop the restraint and detachment to learn in bite-size intervals, to ask and answer questions in regularized slots during the day, is the man who has learned to deal with himself, his fellow men, and his institutions with restraint—that is, in bite-size intervals of efficient, if not repressive, tolerance.

The present university does not care about community within it, although its leaders often pay lip service to community. The bureaucratic style does not make it easy for community to develop. The university does not care about life in its dormitories. It has emasculated student attempts to build their own institutions by limiting either the power of those institutions or their financial resources. The university classroom builds a vertical relationship between students and the professor, who imparts wisdom from the lectern, without attempting to build horizontal relationships between students or to expand the context of relationships between students and professors. The grading system contributes to competitive rather than communal learning, as does the system of honors and awards presumably designed as incentives for learning.

The ideology of many of those who run universities makes one suspect that they fear community when it develops. Liberal administrators often assume that an attempt to decide on a matter of public concern by majority vote of the public will deny the civil liberties of the minority. Certainly this assumption is basic to the response of administrators to the possibility of a university commitment to a particular position. In fact, however, I have found the exercise of civil liberties to be greatest in periods when communities, whether university or public, face difficult public choices. Furthermore, institutions are not static and a matter is not permanently settled by voting on it once.

That the administrator may want his institution to be static, to be orderly, will not make it so. The minority will always try to exercise its liberties in the hope that the current majority will be shifted. Educational leadership does not believe that this process will occur, or does not want it to occur, even when it contributes to the exercise of those liberties which neutrality is supposed to protect. What is expressed in this stance, apart from its static view of institutions, is fear of community, and one need only look at the university's major components to see that this fear is built into every one of them.

The university is loyal to the dominant institutions and values of society. The university's special purpose and dimly perceived traditions permit some internal deviations from the cultural norms, yet even those deviations are tolerated more than encouraged by the institution. Often, as Shoben notes, they are not even tolerated.

In general, university leaders embody the ideals of their institutions—they are receptive, in the manner of photographic plates with only a mild chemical mixture to give contour to incoming data. This receptivity is directed at both the internal and external communities. Consequently, the exercise of strong will, loud voice, rational persuasion, and, yes, power by components of the internal community will often shift the institution's policies toward new views which deviate from those of the predominant society. Those within the university who wish to transfer patterns of loyalty in this manner, however, must often fight to do so, just as minorities in the larger society must fight to transfer the resources of government.

Until recently, universities viewed direct action and activism as having no part in the learning process. However, a few institutions have developed community action programs which integrate academic research with experience in the field. By and large, though, universities have resisted such programs on the assumption that they violate the institution's traditional processes for conducting affairs and their established approaches to learning. The university's unwillingness to incorporate action programs into the curriculum is often attacked as a separate problem. It is better viewed as one part of higher education's peculiar view of subjective experience. The academy denies the validity of subjective experience. Its purpose has been to enable its members to stand aside from subjective experience and comment upon it.

More often than not, however, standing aside comes to mean repressing. "Value judgment," "that's just your opinion," "I don't care what you do with the material in this course," are familiar professorial rejoinders to a classroom ideologue. The problem is not simply that facts and values are confused. Often, the difficulty which students face springs from the academy's attempt to handle both facts and values as if they had no personal relevance to students. Instead of encouraging the student to employ a variety of theoretical apparatuses in order to clarify his experience, the university urges him to use a style which denies any substantive relationship between experience and thought. As Friedenberg notes: "The shift toward empirical dominance, then, has been a social and political as well as technological and epistemological shift. . . .

Yet all this has a Gresham's Law type of effect, for empirical knowledge is, in some ways, worse knowledge than the kind it replaces. Its very scorn of inwardness and subjectivity makes it, by definition, finally unconvincing; one is not even allowed to raise the question of conviction about it—to doubt that which has been, for all practical purposes, proved."[2]

Ultimately, this epistemology may inhibit, rather than enhance, certain kinds of understanding. Surely the essence of realizing the greatness of a novel or play lies in becoming involved with its drama, its conflicts, its tensions. Such involvement is impossible if the student must approach the work as a dissectable corpse, and I have had many fine pieces of literature killed by that approach. To understand the plight of the poor or of the black people in this country, is it not essential to attempt to put oneself in the position of being poor or black—to play the other person's role? The university urges students to see the other side, but only as an observer, not as an empathizer. In denying the validity of subjective experience, the university makes it impossible for students to clarify their own lives, or those of other people. Black students demanding black studies programs taught by black people have been making this point to our universities, and the begrudging manner in which the college administrations and faculties agree to their demands indicates their inability to handle this kind of epistemology.

The dispassionate approach to inquiry, which encourages the student to stand back from his experience, has had another effect on university curricula—the elimination of traditional theory courses. Until recently, for example, philosophers ignored courses on the fundamental questions of their tradition, preferring to deal with approaches developed since Wittgenstein. It has only been since the new left has been raising fundamental ethical and moral questions in the university community that the philosophy departments are beginning to return to them.

Similarly, political theory is no longer a prerequisite to a major in political science. Traditional sociological theory is ignored

[2] "Truth: Upper, Middle and Lower." In *Dignity of Youth and Other Atavisms* (Boston: Beacon, 1965), p. 29.

by many sociologists and their students. A friend of mine at the University of Chicago despaired recently of his educational background, stating, "There's no one left who can talk to me about such matters." In relation to the collapse of theory, traditionalists, like Jacques Barzun, and new left intellectuals, like Carl Oglesby, come together. Both understand that the construction of alternative social orders requires facility in handling fundamental theoretical questions.

It is the nature of such speculation that it leads to no one answer. One may ask what a particular theorist says about a particular issue, as do most courses which still consider theory and theorists. As soon as you ask whether what he says is true, however, you are stuck. The methods of answering questions concerning limited aspects of the world fail us here and there is no alternative methodology to provide even a probable answer. Where is the technique to determine the nature of man or the nature of justice or the nature of the good life? The answers to such questions must be subjective, yet subjective considerations are uncomfortable for the analytical professor, who has no basis on which to evaluate them. Theory courses are therefore dropped from the program.

Consequently, the fundamental issues which students have been exploring are ignored in the classroom. Students have realized that liberal ideology no longer provides a coherent explanation of the way the world works or the way it should work. Yet the so-called behavioral studies are built upon liberal epistemology and theory; the social sciences are dominated by liberal analysts; the humanities have adopted a humane scientism as the appropriate methodology for consideration of art. Without any intensive exposure to men who have treated the university's closed philosophical questions as open ones, students must fish around for people, such as Noam Chomsky, who analyze the world from an alternative framework or for theorists, such as Marx, who have at least provided a powerful political alternative to the liberals, if not the best theoretical alternative. I blame these trends on academia's failure to take seriously the nature of subjectivity or the kinds of questions subjective man wants to answer.

Friedenberg suggests that the denial of subjectivity has had social and political consequences as well as technological ones. I agree. Men who cultivate detachment lose the ability to understand why a particular preference may be of enormous importance to someone. Sustained detachment, moreover, leads to the development of political attitudes such as that one must consider an issue on its merits, when, in fact, the issue is relevant only insofar as the way it is resolved will help one group or another. Other results of detachment are the Aristotelian notion that in any conflict both sides are partially right and the notion that the just state is that which provides rules for the adjudication of conflict in an orderly fashion, without concern for the way in which conflict is resolved.

Indeed, maintaining an objective stance, retaining distance from the "petty partisan battles" which divide men, has become the one vested interest for which university men will fight. Many become uncomfortable when the nature of their loyalties is questioned; most refuse to permit their institutions to attach themselves to any group of men except those who value detachment. (They refuse to believe that any commitments the university does make involve political decisions.) When a professor tells a student radical that certain actions are never appropriate he states a political position—a position which protects those who fear making choices from having to do so. Hitler may rise; Joseph McCarthy may wreak havoc in the nation, but it is only when such men and movements threaten the professor's cherished detachment that he speaks out against them. Slums in the surrounding community and bleeding peasants in Vietnam have been assailed by a few within universities, but the institutions and the majority of their faculties preserve their cherished detachment rather than sully their objectivity in a messy political battle. Alinsky summed the matter up well in 1946:

Liberals in common with many conservatives lay claim to the precious quality of impartiality, of cold objectivity, and to a sense of mystical impartial justice which enables them to view both sides of an issue. Since there are always at least two sides to every question and all justice on one side involves a certain degree of injustice to the other side, liberals are hesitant to act. Their opin-

ions are studded with, "but on the other hand." Caught on the horns of this dilemma they are paralyzed into immobility. They become utterly incapable of action. They discuss and discuss and end in disgust.[3]

Their disgust is that of the man who fears his ability to feel, who is uncertain of his loyalties in the surrounding society, and who, as a consequence, resists intensive conflicts which force him to choose.

The present university is dispassionate, analytical, free, noncommunal, objective, impartial, tolerant, competitive, loyal to the dominant institutions and processes of society, flexible enough to listen to a dissenting opposition and even to grant a few of its demands, determined to retain its neutrality and maintain internal relations which make it easy for its citizens to remain neutral. It has not produced Nazis—indeed, studies show that students emerge from such institutions a bit more tolerant and liberal than when they enter. Yet after a decade of liberal domination, a decade in which tolerance has come to include sustained tolerance of a war in Vietnam (until both the Vietcong and the radicals in the United States showed the liberals that life would become quite more uncomfortable as long as the war continued), tolerance of nonenforcement of civil rights legislation, tolerance of a regressive tax structure, and tolerance of inadequate measures to combat social ills. The creation of such tolerant men is no longer, as Robert Kennedy would put it, satisfactory. We need men with the toughness of the new vision.

How can we build educational change? Is it impossible to transform the present university into the new university? Will transformation of the university contribute to a broader social and political transformation of society? Is it possible even to discuss serious change in present institutions of higher learning? Must those who seek a new vision create an entirely new institution? Certainly, when one talks to liberals, one gets that impression. Often I have heard even sympathetic presidents of colleges or chairmen of departments tell me that they would love to do something, but, but, but, and that our only hope lies in the creation of new institutions.

[3] S. Alinsky, *Reveille for Radicals* (New York: Vintage, 1969), p. 20.

Bruno Bettleheim has led this response, pointing out that radicals who do not like current educational institutions can leave them.

This liberal response, based on fear of the conflicts which arise when people get serious about change, ignores a major political concern of radicals. The epistemology of the university not only debases the experience of the student, it also renders him incapable of developing the commitment and toughness needed to fight for the underclass here and abroad. Objectivity is a stance of moral confusion. If a radical allows the schools to inculcate that stance into their students, he is being irresponsible to those for whom tolerance of racism means its continuation, for whom fairness with employers and businesses who want tax loopholes means sustained poverty. In short, the radical cannot leave. Even when he hates his university, he must stay to fight it, to create converts for the movement.

The question becomes not whether to work for change, but how? Radicals disagree. Members of SDS have developed one model; radicals in NSA are exploring an alternative. Their objectives are the same. To explore the question of how, one must understand the goals and what each of the strategies entails.

Three objectives are involved in moving from the present university to the projected one. First, a student must become part of a community in which he shares and absorbs a learning process which builds around his real feelings, his expanding desire to aid other members of the group, and his commitment to cultural pluralism. The community experience both breaks down the student's fear of other people and offers a cultural and social milieu within which ideological defenses of privatized liberty and glorification of the acquisition of personal goods and property at the expense of relationships with other people begin to seem foolish.

Second, as the student's commitment to building a feeling, expanding, cohesive community grows, he must share the experience of those in the culture for whom community is impossible. A student must see the world through black eyes or through the eyes of a Vietnamese peasant whose village has just been bombed or through the eyes of a white farmer in Appalachia. If the community experience itself will begin to discredit ideologies of privatism, the building of loyalties to those who suffer will fuel the fires which demand that our institutions and people become committed to communal goals.

Finally, the student must develop the toughness and skills to combat the forces, the institutions, and the people whose beliefs and behavior make both community and cultural pluralism impossible. The toughness is built in real battles for institutional change. The skills are built through hardheaded consideration of the theories which our institutions use to justify themselves, the interests which are served by them, the ways in which they use power and in which power supports them, the techniques by which men have changed and can change, and the social, moral, and technical resources needed to build a new social order. Every conversation between movement people concerning objectives and strategies revolves around generating these energies on the campus. The main disagreement is over the best way to reach these objectives.

SDS believes that fighting universities involves exposing their real constituencies in the outside community, demanding that they sever connections with the most pernicious institutions in the society, and fighting for an institutional commitment to build programs under community control for the benefit of the poor, the black, and the Vietnamese. If demands which the students support or can be made to support are made upon the institution and if those demands are built around issues of importance to blacks and Vietnamese, and if the university rejects the demands—responds violently to those who make them—then the liberal student will lose faith in the university and become radicalized.

Columbia's rebellion was conceived precisely in this fashion. The radicals made demands and took radical action to prove their willingness to fight for them. In taking over buildings, they built several subcommunities in confrontation, whose internal processes are built around democratic principles and whose cohesion strengthens as the confrontation continues. Importantly, the communities in the building force the detached students to choose. Although many refuse to do so, try to chart a middle course, or even support the administration, they gradually come to accept the protesters' demands, if not their methods. When the university calls in the police, who obligingly behave like police, students turn against the institution and ally with the left. In terms of realizing the three objectives of the new university quickly, the Columbia revolt could not have been more successful.

Yet there were and are several problems with the Columbia model. The most obvious problem is how to build upon the revolution once it succeeds and once the students have united around the left. Columbia's rebels tried, but they could not develop a coherent and transformed university on the spot to which the students could gravitate for a new kind of learning experience built around their needs. Eric Mann, SDS organizer, expressed some sense of the problem in a speech to the one thousand who were arrested: "We're developing the same problems here which those of us who worked in Newark began to develop. We constructed brilliant tactics to delegitimize the institutions, even to build a community of insurgents. Yet once we succeeded, we did not know how to sustain the momentum." In notes I wrote at the time, on May 4, 1968, long after classes had been suspended, I made a similar observation:

The dynamic builds toward the logical pronouncement that the liberated university of Columbia has been established, that it will function through the month, it will run classes, it will discuss its structure, it will maintain resistance against the old university, it will exist regardless of the administration's acceptance of any demands. . . . Yet those who build a strike, who create the transformed university from the strike, remain trapped both by the rigid words of their platform and their own horror at gazing into the chasm which lies before them, which they must fill. A militant—"we must press harder on our position." An observer—"We need another escalation, a new mass action against the administration." The irony is that a new escalation, a new mass action against the administration, will be a retreat—a retreat from the building of the transformed university back into the process of challenging the old university. Yet it will be called an escalation. No one will understand.

The Columbia rebels never did build a new university at

Columbia. Nor has the university itself developed the resources for reconstruction along any lines, let alone radical lines. Liberals could not be expected to accomplish the task; radicals were not interested in doing so. Consequently, even though the university no longer involves itself with the Institute for Defense Analysis (IDA) or unilaterally builds a gym in the ghettos, it has made few strides toward a permanent radicalization which SDS members might appreciate.

In a way, however, Columbia was a brilliant success. It did generate a new dynamic in the institution for several weeks, one which created an enormous amount of thought and talk, personal change, and social inquiry at the institution in succeeding months. It has sped up the process of institutional change elsewhere in the country. Although the revolution did not maximize its real possibilities, it went a long way.

I do not, however, favor beginning a process of university reconstruction with takeover like that at Columbia, even if the participants understood how to move once the takeover has been accomplished. Columbia's radicals were lucky—the administration did call in the police, the police did act like police. If neither had happened, the whole business would have failed. When the police arrived, a compromise proposal was developing within two of the five buildings. It was the university's own blundering which enabled the radicals' predictions to come true.

Unlike those Marxists who believe that the capitalist class will respond violently whenever attacked, I believe that university liberals can develop the skills of self-preservation just as corporation liberals can. Morris Abram has shown the way at Brandeis: wait the rebels out, give in on less important demands, unite the forces opposed to insurgency quickly so that the question becomes order or disorder, rather than students against the corporate structure, refuse to call in the police, and appear reasonable at all times. Insurrection aimed at winning support from an apathetic majority of students can be and will frequently be thwarted easily by liberals in this manner.

The methods of the radicals in the NSA make more sense. None of us eschews confrontation. Yet we believe that one must build a base of insurgent students who control, or who can control, the majority of the student body before insurgency against the administration can be effected. A union organizer does not call a strike until the workers support him. We are trying to construct environments which give us support.

The first step toward that support is to start the conversation of insurgency. This is the sort of conversation I described earlier in connection with the new university. The conversation may be called an experimental college, a commune, or a cooperative. The label is less important than the message it telegraphs to the student body—a group of people are trying to break alienation, isolation, and privatism by conducting a new kind of learning experiment within the university. An alternative is provided to the students which initially can be explored by them with minimal risks.

Since most students are lonely, angry at their classrooms, bored with their courses, unsure why they came to college, any alternative which appears attractive will be supported. If the insurgents have developed a healthy conversation, it should involve quite a few students in a short time. I have seen this process develop brilliantly at Chapel Hill, Duke, Dartmouth, Newton College of the Sacred Heart, and many other supposedly moderate or conservative institutions, in addition to places like San Francisco State and Oberlin.

The second step is to build into the experimental college, or urge black students to build into their program, some activity which forces students to confront the black struggle seriously. In some cases this confrontation can come through a community action project in which students participate initially out of a sense of guilt, but which begins to show students that winning real change for black people involves real personal risks and battles. In some cases, blacks can demand that the university institute programs in the blacks' behalf. In others, black students may instill in white students a consciousness of black issues and then get white students to support their demands. Whatever the process, if the new communities are to be more than simple interchanges of interpersonal growth, if the new communities are to relate to the broader task of building economic justice and cultural pluralism, then students must be made to view the world through black eyes.

The third step is to encourage every student to begin to challenge the institution. Often the first challenge develops around issues of immediate student concern. Radicals should not avoid such issues. Indeed, if they ally themselves with the mass of students on trivial concerns like student social rules and the quality of the food, they will gain credibility for when they seek support for their challenges on more basic aspects of the institution. Anything which identifies a radical with a healthy change in the university which students support is to the radical's advantage; anything which demonstrates to the students that the institution is slow to change, even in response to simple student demands, builds a sense that the insurgent university is needed.

The fourth step is to begin, through rhetoric, through conversations in the community, and through articles in the school newspaper, to build a theoretical framework which connects the experience of the experimental college, the needs of black people, and the resistance of universities to student power in a coherent fashion. Whenever I have presented my analysis of these relationships, it has made sense to students.

The fifth step is for the organizers to galvanize their new constituencies around demands which will shift the old university to the new. These demands would include demands for student power over student life, and student participation in faculty decision-making. They would include elimination of grades, academic credit for projects developed by the new communities within the university, and the development of community action curriculum projects to meet the needs of the black community.

The demand would reach into the classrooms to ask professors who are bad lecturers why they continue to lecture and to ask why courses are built on certain models. If a professor wanted to limit discussion to an analysis of what the course material said, students would press for discussions into which their own real feelings could be injected. The battle for curricular change would be fought within each classroom rather than simply on committees which might change the formal structure of the curriculum but not the process by which it is disseminated.

The demands would challenge the social content of both the courses and the university itself. Physical scientists would be asked, as they have been at MIT, to explain why they research what they do and for whom. Social scientists would be asked to devote their methodological skills to questions which groups in the community were asking. While the right to conduct certain kinds of research would not be challenged, its wisdom would be.

The new communities would move hard to infect the dormitories and the lounges, the informal settings where students and faculty gather. They would urge the university's funding institutions to transfer resources to their new programs. They would raise serious question about the traditional ways in which the university spent and invested its money. They would organize to shift the institution's political emphasis to the needs of the underclass and its educational emphasis to those students committed to aiding the underclass, building new communities, and working toward cultural pluralism.

Each of these suggestions has appeared elsewhere; many have been tried successfully. The important point about this process is that it involves a variety of efforts to change first the context within which students view their university, then the theory which connects the components of their reality to the reality around them, then the spirit with which they approach the possibility of institutional change. Whether the process involved confrontation and violence would depend upon the response of the institution to specific demands. If the students developed a sense of transforming an old community into a new one, bringing the old university to terms with the new university which had already developed within it, then confrontation would be a device to influence the administration and faculty, not a necessary instrument for organizing the students themselves. Marx noted that revolution is the midwife of an old society pregnant with a new one. If he is correct, then the transition between old and new universities may require violence. The responsibility for violence would lie with the institution's intransigence, not with the students' premeditated design.

Will the cultural and epistemological transformation of the university contribute to the building of a new political consciousness? Is the university the best place for a new political consciousness to be developed? If the efforts to change universities will make little political difference, as a few revolutionaries suggest, or if there are better places to start, as angry administrators claim, then those of us who call ourselves educational radicals are barking up the wrong picket sign as it were.

I believe that the changes in universities I have outlined will build new political consciousness. Contrary to the socialists' belief that rational presentation of a program will persuade an intransigent opponent, most studies of politics indicate that views emerge from a context of cultural and social experiences. I have tried to show a few important connections between culture and politics in both the new and old university. One does not need much training in sociology or political science to learn that most Jews vote Democratic, that most upper class people vote Republican, or that Progressives developed a set of demands concerning political institutions which corresponded to their cultural style.

If students can be immersed in a community environment which provides an enriching and challenging experience, which tests their loyalties, their abilities to feel, their willingness to take risks to achieve change, then they will begin to view all social and political institutions in a new way. Communalism makes sense only to those who do not fear community, who are not trapped by a psychology which makes libertarian appeals both ethical and satisfying. Cultural pluralism can be built only when people begin to want to absorb new experiences and environments. A demand to change the nature of the public institutions of the country can emerge more easily if the student has learned that he can challenge the institutions of learning around him. As an example of all these points, I offer my alma mater, Oberlin College, where during the sixties students created a new university of such strength that even those who enter as conservative Republicans leave as liberals or radicals and stay that way.

Possibly the task could be accomplished elsewhere, but it would be harder. The university is the one institution in society in which questions of learning, growth, being, commitment, loyalty, and change are at least asked, and asked in the context of the institution's own traditions. One could not ask those questions in a corporation, in a union, or in a political party. This does not mean that present universities are better than other institutions of the society. In fact universities are probably fulfilling their traditional functions less adequately than other institutions. The creation of the mechanisms for personal, interpersonal, social, political, and cultural transformation should be the goal of the university, not a threat to it. That I can make this statement indicates why the university is an institution ripe for radical organizing. It is not that its operations are vulnerable or fragile, as liberals charge. It is that its traditions are radical, conducive to radical change.

The transformation of the university will not bring in its wake the immediate reawakening of the social order. Yet it will be an important first step, as what the universities do to students now is important. As young people emerge from different sorts of socializing institutions and attempt to find roles for themselves in the places which the society has built, they will have to fight for change in order to stay alive. Already what we have done has had an effect. I can think of no area of national life which has not been altered by student demands, many of which emerged through involvement in some aspect of educational change.

Consequently, we battle to build the new university. Whether our battle will involve a revolution depends upon the institutions themselves; we are not afraid to start one. We recognize the risks, but we think they are worth taking. At this point, the state of humanity is much too serious to be left to the humanists.

PART THREE

THE NEW CONSCIOUSNESS

Paul Spike

Phenomenology of Today's Students

VIII

Born in 1947, I am an undergraduate at Columbia University in New York City. Since I am not a sociologist, an educator, a campus minister, or even an acknowledged spokesman for my fellow students, this chapter is necessarily a little peculiar. That is, I would be hard pressed to choose a category into which it can fit easily. My qualifications to speak are really only my particular point of view and a willingness to risk publishing that opinion. My home for four years has been one of America's most complicated and unusual college campuses, Morningside Heights. Living there has been, as college catalogs love to say, an education beyond the classroom. I hesitate to call what I have learned facts. Nor are they really values.

I suppose, preferring the risk of being simpleminded to that of being inaccurate, I would call what I have learned simply what I now know.

Any discussion of today's students ought first to note that there are more students today than ever before and that they are generally better educated than their predecessors. Probably an average student not only thinks he knows more than his parents, but actually does. However, parents have always felt confident of their authority in the past because of the greater experiential knowledge they possessed. Not so today. My generation is the first to be in the rather frightening position of being able to refute this notion of adult experiential superiority. American society and culture have changed so enormously, technology has come so far into the space age, that what I am saying is not as totally irresponsible and as wild as it once would have been. For I believe that experience (outside of the most basic facts—birth, death, suffering, joy) garnered in the years preceding World War II is now too often irrelevant and quite inadequate as background for today.

My generation's parents were a very optimistic generation. They were the surviving children of the depression, the victorious young men of World War II. This is the generation now in Washington, and in Low Library and Sproul Hall. There has always been a power struggle between generations, but what we have today, a generation gap if you care to call it such, is new. There is probably less respect for one's elders today than ever before and sons will hardly give lip service to their fathers' achievements. A small but growing minority of today's young people are telling their parents, in a fantastic role reversal appropriate to such fantastic times, to either shape up or ship out. Parents, utterly amazed, often call in the police to restore order.

The children of great optimists, we are super-optimists. We feel our ideals must be fulfilled, by any means necessary, whereas to our parents, ideals merely ought to be fulfilled. We are super-optimists and consequently super-cynics. We wonder aloud whether our parents' survival during the depression, of which we are often reminded, was good preparation for today's world, which holds the shuddering possibility of nuclear overkill. We are super-cynics who wonder if the optimism our parents won in World War II may not cripple them in the middle of the cold war. And we poke fun at our parents' rigid patriotism and question their ability to comprehend the dangers of nationalism in a world which cannot survive another world war.

We are strange pioneers. A new frontier has been crossed in our lifetimes. The line beyond which most men cease to desire an ever more efficient, ever more comfortable material life may have been reached. The great Western tradition of social mobility and success, of "making it," is drawing to a reluctant close. Many of us feel that "giving our sons what we never had" is absurd for, in material terms, we have had enough for any man. The point now is to give such life to every man. America is littered with monuments to hedonism: Las Vegas, Hollywood, shopping centers, status symbols, enough to strain the imagination. In this huge glittering pile alienation is rampant. It is the cancer of my generation and, perhaps, of the future.

Technological progress has altered our consciousness in ways beyond just a general satiation with fabulous affluence. The speed with which all kinds of change, predictable or unimaginable, take place today, and the rate at which they are reported through the mass media have affected our minds. Our parents have lived under the same conditions and have had to adapt to them, but they have not, for example, sat in front of a television from infancy. We know nothing from our own experience but a world which contains the possibility of overkill. We know nothing but a world in which facts appear with dizzying speed: Sputnik, Suez, Vietnam, the Arab-Israeli conflict, pot, STP, and the new 1970 Buick.

In the twenties, T. S. Eliot modernized poetry with his abrupt transitions from line to line without traditional linkings of ideas and descriptions. What Eliot did in his poetry is now part of our everyday thinking. It is only when one is writing a term paper or talking to someone in an official capacity that he bothers to build the old intellectual bridges in his writing and speech. Young people are often accused of incoherency and sloppiness. In the books of William Burroughs, the poetry of John Ashbery, the songs of Bob Dylan, the movies of Jean-Luc Godard, there is a common esthetic presumption which both escapes and infuriates those who approach art in traditional fashion. The new art is nonlinear. It rebels against plots and narratives and in their place emphasizes fragmentation, juxtaposition, and speed.

Our technology has made not only material affluence but also spiritual affluence too easily attainable. Consider, for example, the failure of traditional American churches to win respect or support from today's students. The percentage of students at prestige schools (the ones which reject far more students than they accept for admission) who are active in church activities must be incredibly small. Aside from an annual barrage of action projects, the traditional denominations in this country seem to be losing their battle to bring the church into the world and establish its relevance to modern existence. The young have rejected Western spirituality. The Eastern modes of meditation, withdrawn observation, and ecstatic enlightenment, all of which require great devotion and discipline, seemed to be invading America in the late fifties through the beat and Zen movements. But events have dealt them a fatal blow, at least in the West, through the growing use of drugs. Our laboratories can now provide in capsule form, legal or illegal, almost any variety of heightened or lowered experience one might desire. All that is missing is the devotion and the discipline of Eastern tradition, and yet, to the contrary of our Puritan ethic, the results of drugs are apparently the same as Eastern enlightenment.

The bomb and its effect upon my generation must also be considered. It is understandable, I suppose, that one of the quickest ways to provoke members of the older generation into violent scoffing and dissent is to mention the bomb to them. Time after time, when emphasizing the effect of the bomb on us, the first post-Hiroshima generation, I have heard: "Don't tell me you are worried about that! What do you people do all day, sit around and feel sorry for yourselves? Worry about the world being blown up? Get serious!"

The fact is that the world could be blown up and that very possibility changes man's consciousness to an immeasurable extent. I have friends who have recurring dreams in which nuclear catastrophe or World War III symbolizes anxiety and depression. The effect upon our culture of this most dramatic technological fact of all time, man's capacity to destroy all his past and all his future, must necessarily be immense in the light of what we know about the interdependence of technology and ideology. The possibility of such great violence explains why the dominant anxiety among many students is no longer expressed in sexual feelings but in feelings of aggression and fear of losing control of one's hostility. This has been observed by Erik Erikson and Kenneth Keniston.

The violence of the bomb is the same rising violence evident on other fronts, such as city crime rates, ghetto riots, police riots, and the astonishing number of assassinations. It is important for anyone interested in understanding my generation, often called violent and arrogant by our elders, to understand the effect the assassinations have had on us. We were juniors in high school when John F. Kennedy was assassinated. We were juniors in college when his brother Robert and Martin Luther King were assassinated. In the four years between, other leaders who won the respect of my generation were assassinated: Malcolm X, Che Guevara, Robert Spike, Medgar Evers, James E. Chaney, Michael Schwerner, and Andrew Goodman. Psychiatrists have observed that for young blacks in the ghetto what would normally be considered paranoid modes of thought are only healthy. I believe that the same holds true for young white students in political movements. Anyone who has ever seen a police riot, whether at Chicago on television or at Columbia in person, knows it is not paranoid to wear a crash helmet to a march intended to be peaceful.

Of all the violence my generation has seen, the war in Vietnam is the worst. Vietnam is the focus of most student protest. It is now realized that if it had not been for Vietnam my generation would probably not have become politically active so quickly. However, ending the war in Vietnam will not silence the student activist movement. Vietnam has been the greatest textbook my generation has had to study. Chief among the things we have learned is that there is a great gap between our perceptions and our parents'. Vietnam has been the experience about which both generations have taken notes and made predictions. A genuine gap exists between the conclusions and predictions of most students and those of their parents.

It is not simply a matter of being against the war. Students are also concerned about such issues as whether our traditional forms of government are still effective. Eugene McCarthy ran for President to reassert these forms and to repudiate any youthful nihilists who challenged them. But the nihilists' views are too strongly based in current events to be easily repudiated. Vietnam is now the third most violent war in our history, yet it still has not been declared by Congress. It should be deemed illegal on Constitutional grounds. But, in fact, for several years the administration in Washington used the illegality of the war to pacify the nation by claiming that Vietnam was not a real war, just defense against Communist aggression. Such hijinks in Washington have taught students that even though something is corrupt, as long as it is defended on "traditional American" grounds, the older generation will hesitate to question it. Whether or not the Vietnam War is ended soon, my generation is not going to forget the lessons it has taught us, especially its lessons about patriotic rhetoric.

This has been a decidedly gloomy account of influences on my generation. What of the "new vision" and what of our newfound freedom to experiment with life, to enjoy it fully, and to fulfill ourselves? I do not believe there is much idea of a new vision among the young. Whatever vision we have is simply ours and is as old as we are. I do not believe that we share a single vision yet. However, I do see many areas in which the way we see things is radically different from the way our parents see them. One of the chief criticisms made of some of the most radical students is that they have the right enthusiasms and immense energies but no real programs to replace those they would abolish, and the criticism is valid. Hopefully, the new ways in which we see things will lead to one glorious new vision of what the future should be.

What I am really saying is that we have not yet found the answers to personal and social happiness. The hippie experiment, for example, was an attempt to derive such answers from dropping out and establishing new life styles on the fringes of society which would be full of joy and rich with fulfillment. That experiment is just about finished. The Haight Ashbury and East Village neighborhoods have been stripped of their glory. They remain full of young people, but the young people are more desperate than joyful, and they show more of the hunted than of the experimenter on their faces. Meanwhile, underground newspapers have become less communal newsletters and more national political muckraking sheets. Student movements in this country, as anyone who has spent much time working in them knows, are usually too time-consuming to allow much time for experimentation with life styles. It is true that couples live together without getting married and drugs are taken frequently and without guilt. But I believe that what motivates my generation is more a despair with the methods and the facts of the past than a new life-sustaining freedom and joy. When we consider the amount of change during our lifetimes, we cannot help shivering at the specter of a future of ever more rapid change.

Ironically, while technology has created the problem of too much leisure time, it has also created the opposite problem. It seems there is never enough time in the urban environment to get everything done, to keep up with all the news, to maintain all the gadgets. Today there is a real question of how much change and speed, how much technology, the human organism can withstand. This dilemma of our times makes a new vision a necessity. Bits and pieces of such a vision are now coming into view. But no one has yet come close to describing what the total picture will be. There is a great deal of struggle left between us and our salvation. If my generation can maintain its enthusiasm and its energy after its first inevitable big defeat, then we may indeed be the possessors of a unique view.

I have been unfair in referring to my generation for I have been describing only a minority of the members of that group. There is a majority which is not radical or even very political, which is not alienated and would probably disagree with almost everything I have written. These are not the uncommitted Keniston wrote about. They are the committed youth in the junior colleges, in the large state universities, in the majority at most ivy league schools, and in the church schools. Erikson has called these young men and women technologists. He says of them:

As in every past technology and each historical period, there are vast numbers of individuals who can combine the dominant techniques of mastery and domination with their identity development, and become *what they do. Those young people who feel at home in it can, in fact, go along with their parents and teachers—because parents and children can jointly leave it to technology and science to provide a self-perpetuating and self-accelerating way of life.*[1]

Erikson's technologists are the young people the university administrator likes to describe as responsible. Although these students do not consider themselves conservative, they disagree completely with their protesting, alienated brothers, whom Erikson calls the humanists. The humanists challenge the technologists' faith in science by pointing to the bomb, to campus war research, and to napalm in Vietnam; they know that technology has been gravely irresponsible. It has brought the world to the edge of nuclear holocaust. The technologists cannot deny this. However, they know that without their science and its applications, the humanists would never have all this time to protest; they would have to be out working instead of dissenting. Erikson sees in this division the makings of a workable dialectic for the future. He is optimistic.

One may question what the future will be like for the technologists. For as technology, aided by these brilliant young people, becomes more and more advanced, it seems destined to make their aid unnecessary. Will the machines make it possible, even necessary, for everyone to be a humanist?

For the time being, humanists are the minority. Many radicals among them talk of an oncoming revolution—a violent overthrow of traditional American capitalism. They see this as the only possible response to the contrasts they see in the world. They compare the great affluence of white America to the gloom of the ghetto and the poverty of the third world. They compare the optimism of today's parents with the lack of fulfillment and the alienation of today's children. A small handful of radical students believe that the way to resolve the great social problems is to promote constant

[1] E. Erikson, "Memorandum on Youth, Toward the Year 2000, Work in Progress," *Daedalus,* 1967, *96*(3), 864.

turmoil in order to provoke first harsh repression and then, hopefully, a revolutionary response to the repression. Other young people simply drop out into drugs and other forms of self-destruction or retire to communes far from the urban world. Then there is a large group of students who are primarily interested in designing a new university which will be the keystone to a new society. Chapter Seven deals with this approach. But the vast majority of the humanists continue to carry on in their studies, disturbed and confused and committed to an unknown future, anxious to determine that future somehow, and not sure how they ought to do so.

Myron B. Bloy, Jr.

A Spiritual Taxonomy

IX

Max Ways has provided a trenchant analysis of the root problem of higher education today:

On campuses where grave disorders have erupted, faculty committee activity has proliferated; but after a few months this tends to peter out as the professors get bored by details outside their fields. The details are all the more tedious because most faculty members seem to lack any lively notion of where they want the university to go, what they want it to be. In an age when all institutions are in flux, it would be unrealistic or downright reactionary to expect the changing university to achieve a hard and fast definition of its pur-

pose and function. But it does need enough sense of identity to respond more clearly than it has to demands for innovation now being made upon it.[1]

And later, setting the dereliction of the faculty in a larger context, Ways says of them, "It is their drift, their detachment, that poses the tragic threat to the university—and makes the university in its present travail a microcosm of American society."[2] Ways shares the increasingly general recognition that the faculty is the key element in the institutional logjam which characterizes higher education today, but his analysis is unusually perceptive in his recognition that if faculty are to become creative change agents they need to be not only free from their reactionary institutional and intellectual habits but also free for the pursuit of a more lively, more integrated vision of the good life for higher education. Furthermore, he makes the point that the problem of finding an enabling vision is one which characterizes the whole culture and all its institutions, not just the university and its potential change agents. The spiritual character of our culture, materially affluent but starving for a commanding vision, is not unlike that which the prophet Amos predicted for Israel: " 'Behold the days are coming,' says the Lord God, 'when I will send a famine on the land; not a famine of bread, nor a thirst for water, but of hearing the words of the Lord. They shall wander from sea to sea, and from north to east; they shall run to and fro, to seek the word of the Lord, but they shall not find it. In that day the fair virgins and the young men shall faint for thirst' " (Amos 8:11–13).

Although I will be speaking largely of the problem of the university's vision, of what it should be free for, I do not wish thereby to imply that freeing it from its institutional hang-ups is unimportant. Institutions must structure enough internal elbowroom to direct themselves toward fulfilling their commanding visions, but, as Ways suggests, without a vision in the first place the energy necessary for even such minimal restructuring never effectively mate-

[1] M. Ways, "The Faculty Is the Heart of the Trouble," *Fortune,* 1969, *79*(1), 162.

[2] *Ibid.,* p. 164.

rializes. So it seems that even an effective nuts and bolts approach to institutional reform is dependent on the energy released by the spiritual awareness of the ends sought. Reform for what? That is the question we must answer, and the answer must have contagious authenticity if it is to transform our vaunted analytical and methodological skills into useful instruments for change. This observation brings to mind the curiously empty quality of Christopher Jencks and David Riesman's *The Academic Revolution,*[3] by all odds the most ambitious, intelligent, and well-written analysis of higher education in our time. The fault of the book, so frustrating in the light of its scholarly depth and dazzle, is its uncritical acceptance of the now flabby and uncertain liberal vision of higher education. Jencks and Riesman's insouciant acceptance of this faded, no longer empowering vision combined with a meticulous analysis of institutional development is typical of our approach to the trauma of higher education; but now, when such analyses seem to lead to less and less significant reforms, we must search for a commanding vision for higher education which can direct analysis and methodological change to real ends.

We live, however, at the end of one age—a time when our inherited norms no longer have the power to win commitment—and at the formative stage of a new one—a time when the new normative urgencies that are stirring still have not come into focus. The resultant spiritual paralysis, which has for many years characterized higher education, which is, in fact, an affliction of Western culture generally, and which we are now enabled to see more clearly against the foil of student and black protest, is what Nietzsche called "the nihilism of the modern age." In 1954 Ignazio Silone wrote a brilliant analysis of our cultural state based on Nietzsche's perception, and it grows in contemporaneity with each passing day. Silone defines nihilism in the following terms:

In its most common moral aspect, nihilism is the identification of the good, the just, and the true with one's own interest. Nihilism is the deep conviction that there is no objective reality behind faiths and doctrines and that the only thing that counts is success. It is

[3] (Garden City, N.Y.: Doubleday, 1968).

nihilistic to make sacrifices for a cause one doesn't actually believe in although one pretends to. It is nihilistic to exalt courage and heroism independently of the cause they serve—here nihilism equates the martyr with the mercenary. Even freedom can be nihilistic, if it is not at the service of life but is turned into slavery.[4]

Silone seems to see our age as one that lives on an inner emptiness, and hides this state of affairs from itself by continuing to use the traditional language of meaning and purpose; faiths and doctrines, sacrifices, courage and heroism, and even freedom become grotesque, self-deceptive masks when they are not rooted in the fact of man's authentic humanity. The predominant norm is nothing more than an unreflective drive for success. Silone then goes on to describe the difficulty of perceiving and breaking through the spiritual dead end of nihilism:

The great difficulty is that nihilism is not an ideology, is not legislatable, is not something to be taken up in school. . . . It is a condition of the spirit which is judged dangerous only by people who are immune to it or who have been cured of it. But most people are not even aware of it, since they think it is an entirely natural way of existence. "Things have always been that way," they say, "and always will be." Post-Nietzschean and existentialist literature has portrayed for us man's well-known present predicament. It can be reduced to this: every tie between man's existence and his essence has been broken. Existence is bereft of every meaning which transcends it. The human is reduced to mere animal energy.[5]

If we find some merit in Silone's description of our spiritual situation, and I do not see how we can avoid agreeing with its general thrust, how is it reflected microcosmically in higher education? Higher education developed in a period when the ties between man's existence and essence were strong indeed; the trivium and quadrivium were seen as almost transparent windows into the essential order and character of reality. However, a movement begun in

[4] I. Silone, "The Choice of Companions," in *Emergency Exit* (New York: Harper and Row, 1968), p. 112. (First published in 1954.)

[5] *Ibid.*, pp. 113–114.

the Renaissance made it apparent, by the nineteenth century, that higher education's spiritual mission had become not to help men perceive and tune their lives to the nature of things but, rather, to free them from all dogmas of essentiality so that they could become autotelic selves, that is, selves free from any spiritual or moral authority except the individual acquisition of power. Higher education's man of lofty critical detachment was analogous to the self-made captain of industry and the self-sufficient pioneer, and all these types were manifestations of the autotelic self. The tools which higher education developed for its own role in this cultural change were a rigorously analytical approach to knowledge—to its teaching as well as to its discovery—and a thoroughgoing skepticism about all spiritual and moral claims on the self. The academician became a kind of Olympian—master of a seemingly self-generating fragment of knowledge through the analytic tools appropriate to that fragment and protected from the claims of any essentiality, save that of scholarship itself, by a calloused skepticism.

The analytical and detached academic style and the institutions which have developed from it not only were satisfyingly congruent with the isolated, repressed, success-driven self which has been our culture's implicit model of man, but have contributed effectively to the technological revolution created by that culture. In fact, it can be argued that the autotelic self-identity which has grown out of the Renaissance is really a necessary function of man's struggle to dominate a threatening environment and that the shaping of man's intelligence to an intensely analytical and coolly detached instrument is a part of that total purpose. If so, we post-industrial men must certainly applaud the success of the autotelic identity in bringing man's energies to an intense and clear focus on that task. But for all practical purposes, in principle and psychologically, man has overcome the threat of nature and now has the elbowroom and leverage to shape himself to a more authentic identity, one which is less emotionally repressed and more responsive to the great challenge of the age, namely, of living together in a global village.

But it is becoming apparent that the liberation of man's intelligence from every dogma of essentiality has been accomplished at the price of so severely abstracting the self from the full range of human experience that commitment to a commanding vision of authentic life is nearly impossible. The drift and detachment of the university are those of an institution immensely skilled in helping to free man from the physical and metaphysical bondages of his past at the ironic price of rendering him almost incapable of committing that hard won freedom to anything but the rigid continuance of that same defensive task. Thus, the nihilism of the university is that described by Silone when he said, "Even freedom can be nihilistic, if it is not at the service of life but is turned into slavery." The slavery is really of two kinds: on the one hand, as I have suggested, the university, captive of its own liberal identity, seems unable to discover and commit itself to a positive vision of authentic life; on the other hand, this very self-captivity makes it the easy prey of other institutions which conceive their ends more positively, even if those ends are simply cruder versions of the culture's nihilistic condition. Thus, American industry and the Department of Defense have found it relatively easy to treat higher education as part of their own research and development enterprises, and now, even when some universities are attempting to bring their resources to bear on the urban crisis, they invariably do it at the direction of the political establishment rather than with the poor and dispossessed, who often must fight that same establishment in order to win their rights.

The most effective captor of higher education is, however, the prevailing social structure itself, which has made the university an effective instrument of socialization according to its needs. Gibson Winter describes this situation well:

Coercion or violence is used day by day in the universities to impose criteria and even contexts of learning that may or may not be congruent with the modes of inquiry and relevance that are shaping the emerging generation. Coercion is the backdrop of the educational enterprise, because education and preeminently higher education is the tedious, almost endless, obstacle course that has been created by a technological society to screen out its elites.[6]

[6] G. Winter, "Coercion and Counter-Coercion: The Campus Revolt," *Christianity and Crisis,* 1969, *29*(4), 955.

In effect, our colleges and universities are covert finishing schools, giving those who participate in them not only the intellectual tools and certification but also the rhetorical and social skills and contacts for success in a stratified society of haves and have nots. This stratification is tacitly assumed and thereby silently affirmed by the university, positively by teaching a life style which tends to remove students permanently from any communication with or concern for the dispossessed and negatively by so fragmenting the search for truth and the very face of reality that it becomes difficult for the initiate ever to perceive again the actual condition of man in our time. Furthermore, the university is generally unable to perceive its captivity by the power structure of society because the myth of the autotelic self has led it to believe that it is, in fact, free from any value-contamination by the larger society and that it should remain so. It is, in short, deluded.

I remember a talk by a professor of biology, reputed to be a great teacher, in which he related an experience intended to shock the audience about the outrageous ideas of students today. He had been asked by a group of freshmen in one of his university's dormitories to participate in a panel discussion on higher education and when his turn came he told the students that the only way to make the most of their education was to give themselves totally to whatever discipline they chose, to become humble disciples of its objective demands. The students responded with anger, seeing in his advice a cop-out from their larger responsibilities as human beings. One student even went so far as to accuse him of being a neofascist. This, said the eminent professor, was an example of the lack of intellectual discipline of the young; their anger, he felt, was absurd because while he agreed it was important to express concern for the disadvantaged in extracurricular ways, higher education in itself should remain free from particular value commitments. The academic ethnocentrism of this scholar reveals both aspects of the university's captivity: it is the captive of an implicit norm for the self which is no longer responsive to the spiritual need of our time—a norm, moreover, so empty of positive direction that more decisive powers of our culture can bend it to their own ends.

The story also illustrates another of Silone's perceptions concerning nihilism: "It is a condition of the spirit which is judged dangerous only by people who are immune to it or who have been cured of it. But most people are not even aware of it, since they think it is an entirely natural way of existence." A growing proportion of students have been cured of higher education's norm of the autotelic self, seeing in its vision of the isolated and harshly focused self the very face of nihilism. The cure began in the early sixties when SNCC began its civil rights drive in the South. White students from major institutions of higher education in every part of the country joined black students in their sit-ins, freedom rides, and efforts for civil rights. When they came back to their campuses, they were alive in a new way, and other students, who until then had not known how dead their own lives were, found this new life contagious. Those of us who were closely involved with students at that time could see this remarkable spiritual rebirth taking place in scores of individuals. Where the students of the fifties had been referred to as privatized, passive, powerless, and uncommitted, we now began to see more and more students who could be said to have grown toward a universalization of identity. That is, they had discovered that it was possible for their lives to be radically open to the lives of others, especially the dispossessed, and this, they began to realize, was what it meant to be authentically human. Although the new consciousness which is evolving out of this perception is still too unformed to specify with any exactitude, Silone, in his own testament, indicates the kind of conclusions toward which it is moving :

In spite of everything then, is there anything left? Yes, there are some unshakable certainties. These, in my belief, are Christian certainties. They seem to me to be so built into human reality that man disintegrates when he denies them. This is not enough to constitute a profession of faith, but it will do as a declaration of confidence. . . . It is supported by the certainty that we men are free and responsible beings; it is supported by the certainty that man has an absolute need of an opening into the reality of others; and it is supported by the certainty that spiritual communication is possible. If this is so, is it not an irrefutable proof of the brotherhood of man?

This certainty also contains a rule of life. From it is born a love of the oppressed which no historical failure can put in doubt, since no vested interest is involved. Its validity does not depend on success. With these certainties which are fundamental to existence how can one resign oneself to witnessing man's potentialities snuffed out in the most humble and unfortunate? How can one consider moral a life that is deaf to this fundamental commitment?[7]

It is precisely this growing consciousness of the brotherhood of man among the young that is challenging higher education's myth of the autotelic self. The struggle is not merely between doctrines but between assumptions about the nature of the self which are each incarnate in a life style; it is a struggle between culture and counter-culture, as Theodore Roszak has pointed out and as I have tried to develop elsewhere.[8]

If the discrete self of higher education's myth is being fundamentally challenged by the universalization of identity among students, the emotional repression necessary to realize that myth's ideal of the self is also being challenged by a more open, sentient, and holistic life style. This side of the challenge is represented most radically by the hippies, but, as any observer will see, the whole counter-culture is hippie-oriented. Music, poetry, art in various combinations and media, experiments in sexual, familial, and communal relationships, a playful spontaneity, and a serious regard for every level of being are all part of the counter-culture. Some persons argue that the neighbor-love of the political activists of the counter-culture is sharply contrary to the new delight in the self, the self-love, of its more culturally oriented members, but this is not true. The students have instinctively rediscovered the old spiritual and newer psychoanalytic axiom that self-love is a necessary condition for mature neighbor-love, or, to put it another way, that a man, to be authentic, must learn how to love his neighbor as himself. I realize, of course, that the public manifestations of the counter-culture do not always seem to reveal a recovery of the per-

[7] Silone, *loc. cit.*, pp. 126–127.

[8] M. B. Bloy, Jr., "Culture and Counter-Culture," *Commonweal*, 1969, *89*(15), 493–496.

ception that man is made for love. This is so for several reasons: first, any dramatic movement of the spirit always attracts a number of persons who use its life to shore up their own nihilistic drives—they adopt the movement's outer signs but they are really spiritual traitors; second, those of us who have been shaped by the myth of the autotelic self distort what we see because we are secretly fearful of the flamboyant, aggressive, arational passion of love; third, the counter-culture, like every revolutionary movement, is always in danger of unconsciously reflecting the values of the culture with which it is struggling—thus, the spiritual and psychological repressiveness of the traditional myth of higher education is reflected in the political repressiveness one sometimes encounters in the student movement. Despite these warnings, I have no doubt that the certainties of which Silone speaks are also the certainties, the spiritual reality, which implicitly motivate the counter-culture.

It remains now to sketch briefly what higher education might look like if the new spiritual commitment of the young were to shape its life. I realize that a given "objective spirit," to use Hegel's term, can be incarnated in a variety of forms, even though each form will bear a resemblance to others born of the same spirit. My description, therefore, does not claim to be a unique educational embodiment of the new spiritual commitment of the young, but it would, I expect, bear a resemblance to such embodiments.

The traditional categories of knowledge, that is, the disciplines and the traditional structures and styles of teaching and learning, look odd indeed from the perspective of Silone's Christian certainties that men are free and responsible beings, that they have an "absolute need of an opening into the reality of others," that this "spiritual communication is possible," and that, therefore, the "love of the oppressed," those upon whom the denial of spiritual communication is most severely laid, is man's "fundamental commitment." Knowledge should be organized to serve this fundamental commitment, and teaching and learning should be mutual efforts on the part of junior and senior colleagues, students and faculty, to become more effective agents for this mission. This commitment entails not merely applying the existing educational ethos and forms to more socially useful ends but, rather, radically restructuring the ethos and forms to embody that commitment. In fact, the growing attempts to aim the existing educational establishment, with its built-in autotelic commitment, at more socially useful ends have served only to reveal the contradiction between such means and ends. For example, when the Harvard-MIT Joint Center for Urban Studies recently announced receipt of a large grant for research on ghetto problems, the ghetto community of Boston countered with a public announcement that they would henceforth not allow themselves to be used in such research as the means for the scholarly advancement of Joint Center personnel. The black community recognized where the real payoff of such research lay. With the distinction between superficial reform (putting meringue on the garbage pail) and radical restructuring in mind, some possible marks of an educational process shaped by the new commitment of the counter-culture can be listed.

Knowledge would be categorized by critical missions we face in responding to the need of the oppressed: the healing of racism, the equitable distribution of the world's wealth, the restructuring of the corporate power of the nation toward peaceful ends, the creation of a less psychologically and spiritually repressive culture, and so forth. Within these mission-determined categorizations, the traditional disciplines would have an instrumental value in bringing certain habits of mind and pieces of a given puzzle to bear with other habits and pieces of a given problem. As Jencks and Riesman constantly point out, the shape of undergraduate education is now merely a result of the drive of disciplinary professionals to create more disciplinary professionals. But in a mission-oriented education, disciplines would become servants, rather than ends, of the educational process, and the focused study of them would be the province more of some graduate programs than of undergraduate education.

Furthermore, when education is mission-oriented not all of its teachers will be disciplinary savants. After all, who understands the needs of the poor better than the poor, or the effects of racism better than racial minorities? Or, as Lawrence Howard points out in a personal communication, who has grappled more consistently with the growing problem of leisure time than the hard-core jobless, who has more to teach about the joys and sufferings of living in the densely populated urban world of the future than those who presently live in ghettos? In mission-oriented education, disciplinary knowledge, even in interdisciplinary form, is only one of the necessary ingredients.

The new curriculum would also encourage the imagination to be projective rather than retrospective. For example, teams of students and faculty would join in the creation of and, where possible, testing of models for social and cultural alternatives to the present arrangements. The understanding of received knowledge and skills would not, as presently, be an end in itself, thereby tacitly assuming the legitimacy of the status quo, but would, rather, assume instrumental importance for helping to shape the new society and culture.

Finally, although I have chosen here to discuss educational reform in itself rather than the intricate problems involved in the political, social, and economic relations of the academic institution to its environment, the importance of these relations for education should not be overlooked. Many people have pointed out the immediate effect that institutional investments and the acceptance of corporate and government grants have on specific educational policy, but I do not believe it is pointed out often enough that these institutional relations form, in effect, a metaphor of the spiritual assumptions of the institution. Thus, these institutional relations are a kind of invisible curriculum within which the student lives and by which, day by day, his attitudes are subtly shaped. Clearly, if an institution's educational practice is to be shaped by love of the dispossessed, so must its relations with its environment.

But if, as I believe, spiritual communication among free and responsible men necessarily assumes such communication with ourselves too, and if our consequent calling is to love the dispossessed as ourselves, then the curricular picture is even more complex. Just as education to create autotelic selves is dependent on a rigorous training in self-repression, so education to make individuals into neighbors is dependent on guidance in making neighbors, rather than enemies, of our selves. We are clearly in deep water here, but the very nature of love requires us to risk it. Many of Jesus' parables are focused precisely on men who have used the rituals and acts of love for, strictly speaking, self-defensive ends, as a kind of hedge against opening themselves to the power of love; think of the elder son in the story of the prodigal son or of the Pharisee who said, "God, I thank thee that I am not like other men, extortioners, unjust, adulterers, or even like this tax collector. I fast twice a week, I give tithes of all that I get." It is only by accident that good effects can ensue from such men.

What, then, would an educational process look like which is focused not only on preparing students for the external tasks which love of the dispossessed might require but also on helping them to become more open to experience, capable of a greater range of expression, more deeply and securely in communication with themselves, and, in short, more able to accept the personal demands and risks of spiritual communication, of love? For one thing, study of the arts and of literature would see painting and poems more as models and inspirations for one's own expression than as objects for scholarly categorization. A goodly portion of a course in, say, metaphysical poetry would be devoted to writing poems in that style so that one's own expressive range and consciousness would be enlarged by those of Donne and Herbert. The same principle would apply to painting, music, and films. But the greatest barrier to self-awareness in our culture is fear and distrust of our bodies and so the curriculum I propose would place great emphasis on kinesthetic expression; dancing would be as important a requirement as freshman composition. Furthermore, Esalen-type techniques—trust walks, yoga, meditation, nonverbal communication games—would be a regular part of the curriculum. Celebrations, rituals, parades, and chanting would also be part of this scene. It would be understood that the purpose of these activities is basically to expand the range of self-expression and, therefore, of self-understanding; they would be implicitly skeptical of that Cartesian dualism which now severely cramps the lives of all who exist in educational establishments and which emasculates the concept of education itself.

It would be further understood that the personal dimensions of spiritual communication, with oneself or others, can be learned only in a community which includes a variety of life styles, including especially those which at any given time are in fact expanding man's consciousness. Educators often say that the purpose of higher education is to expand the consciousness of man, but what they really mean is to extend the consciousness of man in the severely limited terms of the Enlightenment. In our time the most exciting expansion of consciousness is the black consciousness movement. Black Americans, through the distance from the dominant culture that their hate established, through their ability to dissemble, through their marginality to the economic system, have been able to carefully husband a life style, a culture, which is a real alternative to the dominant, so-called middle-class, culture. Black culture is being celebrated by its constituents and any educational community which is not at pains to bring all its members into a learning relationship with this culture is derelict in its responsibility. The experience of cultural pluralism is a necessary ingredient in preparing persons for spiritual communication, for love.

One final point. Whenever a proposal to restructure the university according to certain values is brought up, academic conservatives see in it a threat to academic freedom. Such a threat has been imputed to this proposal, and so it is important to respond to it directly. As I have previously indicated, the freedom of the academy is a relative matter since no human institution exists without normative sanctions. The important questions concern, rather, which sanctions are most appropriate for higher education at a given point in history and whether their application leaves sufficient room for deviance. The isolated, success-driven, repressed self-identity which has shaped the socialization and intellectual processes of traditional higher education has, in fact, served man well in his drive to subdue and turn to his purposes a threatening natural world, but, we are beginning to see, this end has been accomplished at great spiritual cost. Although a certain ethnocentric delusion still prevents many educational leaders from seeing the often brutal intolerance of traditional higher education for deviance from its normative sanctions, the spiritual rebellion of the counter-culture has begun to provide the necessary foil for their enlightenment. The content of this spiritual rebellion—what I have called youth's recovery of the perception that man is made for love, for a shared rather than isolated identity, for a whole rather than a repressed psyche—is also, in fact, much more responsive to the critical needs of man today, which are the creation of an equitable world community and the development of a more fulfilling style of life. Finally, as normative sanctions for higher education, the spiritual assumptions of brotherhood and expressiveness are hardly likely to be more coercive than the existent ones of competitive individualism and self-repression.

Although this brief sketch is anything but adequate as a well-fleshed and structured picture of an educational alternative, it may be enough to suggest the contours which higher education would assume if it incarnated the spirit of expressive brotherhood rather than that of the autotelic self. My belief is that regardless of the weight one assigns to the particular conclusions of the foregoing analysis, this kind of analysis is a necessity for the reform of higher education. Without some clarity concerning the spiritual assumptions embodied in the present system of higher education we remain hopelessly naive concerning our condition, and without clarifying alternative assumptions and the forms they might take we lack the concrete vision to guide and test our efforts at reform.

Lawrence C. Howard

Black Consciousness and Identity Crisis

Black consciousness may point the way out of the deepening crisis confronting higher education. The identity crisis arises largely from the strains associated with the postindustrial, technetronic (technology plus electronics), or mechanized society. The university appears undecided about whether to serve people or the growing machine power. The resulting ambivalence has produced an identity crisis in which it appears that higher education desires primarily to serve itself. Critics urge the university to make a clear choice of man or machine. They declare that higher education must foster a new freedom for man or it will inadvertently cooperate in his enslavement.

Black consciousness comes in, superficially, because black students are prominent in campus disturbances. At a deeper level, blacks' demands that higher education be made more relevant to blacks have taken on meaning for other (minority) oppressed groups on the campus (Puerto Ricans, Chicanos, Indians) and beyond the campus in impacted inner cities, among the isolated rural poor, and abroad under colonial domination. Most significantly, the black critique uncovers how the oppressors oppress themselves.

Oppression is the enemy against which black consciousness struggles. The attitudes and acts which dehumanize blacks have long been obvious, but the present crisis brings out that many non-blacks suffer as if they were (are) black. Postindustrial society threatens most men with oppression. Against these dehumanizing forces, black students offer their consciousness of their blackness. By accepting themelves, the black students have generated enough self-love to allow for greater other-love. Eldridge Cleaver has suggested as much: "The price of hating other human beings is loving oneself less."[1] To become conscious of blackness is to be concerned first for the human dimension. For blacks, this means replacing antiwhite and negative self-images with pro-people feelings. For man in general, it means preference of human goals to nonhuman priorities. In the sense that consciousness of blackness relates to the reduction of oppression (of men of themselves, of men of other men, or of men by systems and machines), it is a relevant response to the human menace in technetronics.

Linking black consciousness and higher education directs attention to the human possibilities in a black-conscious university. One is led to ask: Could a university with a black agenda of self-identity and universal dignity, a university which considers the oppressed of the world its constituency, creatively utilize our growing technetronic capability and thus eclipse the attendant campus crisis?

[1] Quoted from D. Berrigan, "This Man Is Armed: The Cleaver of Eldridge," *No Bars to Manhood* (Garden City, N.Y.: Doubleday, 1970), p. 149. Berrigan adds: "It is a sentence whose spirit rules his book and helps us to gain a sense of the difference between that hatred which shuts men in cages and the prophetic hatred which from a cage responds to keepers and executioners. We have every reason to believe that Cleaver learned to love and accept himself in prison."

Linking black consciousness and learning, soul and Socrates, appears to raise contradictions. I ask the reader to remain open, to hang loose. Apparent opposites often attract. Let us begin by recognizing conflicting premises: First, the crisis in higher education smolders at several levels, but it is most incendiary where only those who have had little of higher education can perceive it. Second, the technetronic thrust, the larger context for the crisis, threatens human growth; yet it also offers possibilities for continued perfection of man, particularly in his spiritual and moral dimensions. Third, the search for black uniqueness will seek out the universal qualities of man, for celebrating the black soul requires proclaiming the inseparability of the species. In crisis and in contradiction, vision to assist reason is needed. Teilhard de Chardin has written:

Seeing.
We might say that the whole of life
lies in that verb . . .
that is to say in vision . . .
To try to see more and better is not
a matter of whim or curiosity or self-indulgence.
To see *or to* perish *is the very condition laid upon everything . . .*
the mysterious gift of existence.[2]

That vision can resolve is made obvious by Malcolm X, a black-conscious man finding freedom in a multicolored fraternity:

you may be shocked by these words
coming from me
but on this pilgrimage,
what I have seen . . .
forced me to rearrange
previous conclusions
I have been speechless and spellbound . . .
by people of all colors
participating in the same ritual . . .
a spirit of unity and brotherhood . . .

[2] T. de Chardin, *The Phenomenon of Man* (New York: Harper and Row, 1959), p. 31.

people who in America would have
been considered white—
but the white attitude was removed. . . .[3]

This chapter attempts to explain the black vision for the university as an aid to subordinating technetronic culture to the service of men. Much in the future of higher education depends on the black students, more depends on the black conscious university, but most depends upon a growing consciousness of blackness in both whites and nonwhites.

So, much depends on you. You are asked to participate with human compassion as well as rationality. You are asked to react, not just to this text, but to the reflections in verse and rhyme. Blacken a little—the empty white spaces—with your personal reactions, your identity in agreement or disagreement, corrections, or just doodles, but at least a human participation.

The Crisis

Black students are for people
in the college's upheaval.
Against establishments we stand
and so leadership command.
Clearest among our reforms
are people's rights reborn.
Blacks confident as brothers
burst stronger chains on others.

The Challenge

Higher education's crisis
brings out the educated view of the lower . . .
of people.
Universities under siege show up
as elites of merit, rightly (?)
above the masses;
curricula, concerns of the college-cultured
professors, tower as men of power,

[3] Malcolm X, *The Autobiography of Malcolm X* (New York: Grove, 1966), p. 340.

opulence in deference to grounds
and gowns.
The products of the higher learning
too often coopted by the powers.
Resistance, only rhetoric under rules
the systems themselves set up.
It is the unusual and usually untenured
man of letters who measures
his first loyalty to mankind.

The Response

Such statements require analysis and, to be responsible, must be based on facts and not on unsubstantiated opinion. Higher education has its problems, but sweeping generalizations must be avoided, for there are exceptions and intentions. The university is not a welfare program or a service station for society. Its functions are to transmit old knowledge, create new knowledge, and give service based on that knowledge. Above all, the university must retain its knowledge-based integrity.

It is not just a matter of disagreement on particulars. Higher education is threatened with open rebellion. The newspapers report the identity crisis largely in terms of the student revolt (revolution) against college administrations.

problems by the score
are posed by presidents and trustees:
the need for more
professors, endowments, new facilities,
the right to regulate themselves
to be their judge and jury
to serve the city, yes,
but adding, with some fury,
the university as such
must not be asked to do too much.

Hundreds of student revolts have occurred. More are anticipated. Virtually no major institution has escaped. Black students, though less than 3 per cent of college students, sparked this revolution, for essentially conservative goals. Black leadership of students emerged in February, 1961 with the student-led sit-ins, freedom rides, and voter registration drives. The student movement began on predominantly Negro campuses in the South. Howard Zinn has called these black students who later formed the Student Nonviolent Coordinating Committee "the new abolitionists."[4] From today's perspective they could be better described as "the liberators," for in the long run they have contributed more toward freeing white (attitudes?) students than toward abolishing racially based economic and political barriers to blacks. Mario Savio and a host of nonblack students went south to join SNCC or SCLC or ESCRU or the Delta Ecumenical Ministry; to Fannie Hammer or Medgar Evers; or to the memory of Schwerner, Goodman, and Chaney, Jonathan Daniels, or the Birmingham Five. When they returned north (blackened?) they launched the student movement from Berkeley to Columbia which transformed the silent generation of college students into human activists.

The resulting rebellion (liberation) reflects more than acts of activists. *Fortune Magazine* recently suggested that activists articulate feelings held by two-fifths of all students, the thousands (millions) who reject higher education as a means to high status and high-paying jobs and want instead an education which is relevant to their social concerns.[5] Nor is liberation limited to colleges. It may be at least as prevalent at high schools and often explains the dropout. The youth assertion, now in progress, is international and inter-ideological. Student rebellions in process, reactions to recent revolts not yet subsided, or preparations for pending liberation dominate the higher education scene.

Do you agree?

Just beneath the rhetoric of rebellion, crisis takes the form of grievances over governance of institutions. Disagreements abound

[4] H. Zinn, *SNCC: The New Abolitionists* (Boston: Beacon, 1964).

[5] D. Seligman, "A Special Kind of Rebellion," *Fortune,* 1969, *79*(1), 68–69.

on who will be admitted, whose education stopped; how students will relate; who will teach and what will be taught; where knowledge will extend. The wishes of the powerful, the meritorious, the privileged—which have prevailed unchallenged—have now been questioned. There is some logic (justice) in the fact that black students who were seldom admitted, quickly dropped, socially ostracized, not hired, not taught about, and generally unknown, would take the lead.

Higher education is de facto segregated. The university is stuck at the level of *Plessey* vs. *Ferguson,* separate and unequal; not yet at the deliberate speed of *Brown* vs. *Board,* inside but assimilated. It cannot hear pleas that participation replace paternalism, that relevance undermine racism, that unity must go forward to community, and that powerlessness at the status bottom undercuts any top. The university cannot see that there is a crisis. The crisis deepens as the university encounters difficulty in correcting evils in itself that it condemns in others; worse, it discovers that its own corrective efforts exacerbate the color conflict. More blacks are admitted each year, but the percentage of blacks in the national student body declines. The consequences of exclusiveness elicit alarm when the count is made, not at the freshman level, but at commencement. With rare exception white colleges and universities give degrees only to certain white (attitudes?).

(For rebuttal)

Educators, white or Negro, hesitate to see
that their own salvation really could be
embedded in blunt demands by blacks.
Only under duress have educators admitted,
more blacks must be admitted as students,
hired as professors,
added as administrators.

(why must you demand?)
(If they are qualified.)

More attention, many now agree,
must be mustered for
black studies

(If teachers with proper credentials can be found.)

More aid should be extended to the Negro and to the
poor in cities.

(But who will give us the money?)

Belatedly, supporters of education assent
there is a place for the predominantly Negro college.

(If the emphasis is on the predominant.)

Provisionally, and under pressure,
the ethos of expanding opportunity is accepted.

(Coincident with faltering Federal funds.)

But in all, the healing messages are missing.
It is one thing to offer help,
another to recognize that the helper, too, needs help,
a third, to see help helping helpless helpers.
Or in other words,
it is easier to expand opportunities for blacks
than to give blacks the opportunity to expand,
and harder still for whites to take this opportunity
to expand their blackness.

(why must you demand?)

Other grievances which produce crisis reflect restlessness in the governed constituencies. The loyalty of faculties has been drained away from campuses to guilds or disciplines. Students remain alienated, isolated, seeing themselves as wards. The university as an institution is seen increasingly as synonymous with frustration, dependency, indecision, and fear. The governed increasingly feel oppressed. Steps to reemphasize teaching or to relax regulations come across as reluctant responses to symptoms, remedies as empty as compensatory projects, handouts to blacks.

On a deeper level, inadequate responses bring out compromises in higher education. Students criticize the university's choice of companions—the business support which is profit from people privation; they criticize the university as slum landlord and its secret agreements: Camelot, the Institute for Defense Analysis, the corruption of NSA by CIA. As students have probed they have found it hard to find the university's values.

Warren B. Martin has suggested that higher education faces an identity crisis:

personal commitments
of the faculties and administrators
have seemed so malleable or so minimal
that students have often concluded that
a hierarchy of values is unnecessary or impossible.
But life without distinctions is boring,
even as one without meaning is death.
Men cannot live in a value vacuum.[6]

William Arrowsmith similarly projects a normative crisis:

what students want is not necessarily what they need . . .
but we have students concerned to ask the crucial questions
of human existence—identity, meaning, the existence of value,
the good life, and the response to this profound hunger
has been parochial, uncomprehending, or cold.[7]

Closer to the heart of the crisis is concern about the patterns of thought which prevail in higher education, what Bloy has described as a clash between the student culture and the culture of the college:

we should expect the counter-culture to be in conflict with
higher education—that cultural shrine of the Enlightenment.
There is, of course, conflict aplenty,
and it is not simply a conflict over institutional power,
which a little political reorganization will solve,
but a much deeper conflict of opposing cultural assumptions
which takes a great effort of imagination even to grasp.
The traditional intellectual style of higher education
is analytical and morally detached:
it assumes that "truth" is enormously complex but ultimately inert
and that, therefore, an increasingly microscopic and fragmentary

[6] W. B. Martin, "Stalkers of Meaning," *Journal of Higher Education,* 1967, *38*(7), 366.

[7] W. Arrowsmith, "The Future of Teaching," remarks prepared for delivery before the American Council on Education, October 13, 1966.

rationality is needed to unravel it . . .
and that only a strict posture of moral detachment will avoid
compromising its essential inertness.
The counter-culture, however . . . is evolving an integrative
and morally committed style; its members assume that "truth"
is finally unitive (albeit mysterious and alive) and that, therefore,
successively larger, more inclusive perceptions of reality
must be discovered and that only moral engagement
is responsive to its essential sentience.
The clash of cultures here is portentous.[8]

Others, such as Silone, go even further and suggest a certain nihilism in higher education, a product of the university's identification of the good, the just, and the true with its own interests.

The drama of crisis is now familiar.

Councils of education, presidents, and deans,
professors in their disciplines, trustees, legislators,
those charged with education and the silent majority of
students, don't yet expect that blacks have values to offer:
on how to relate to students,
curricular content,
terms of tenure,
reasons for research,
policies for portfolios.
Yet these are the demands that have led
black students to occupy white buildings and Negro ones too.
To present black demands nonnegotiable.

White response: to recognize there is a crisis(?)

To know the pain you must be involved
to feel pressurizing protest join the crowd
Student impatience at administrative inaction,
administrative anxiety at student tactics
the conflict escalates, buildings are occupied,

[8] M. B. Bloy, Jr., "Alienated Youth, Their Counter Culture, and the Chaplain," *The Church Review,* 1968, *26*(1), 12.

confrontation, ultimatums.
The police are called, amid statements of regret,
and when police are resisted
the trauma of troops: tear gas, bared bayonets, bullets, and blood.

The life line of the university collapses into coma.
charge and countercharge, committees, secret negotiations;
the faculty belatedly appears,
debates, and votes
decides—most times—to support black-led demands
backlash ensues and administrations
painfully institute inadequate reforms
still resisting blackness despite the storms.

A crisis is a time of danger
through which individuals and institutions pass,
an illness or a time of preparation,
danger of death or promise of empowered life.
The crisis grows acute when there is no direction
only drift
pitfalls even though seen cannot be avoided
opportunities, though obvious, cannot be embraced.
Higher education is in this suspension, its vitality and
veracity draining out from lack of vision.

"Camus has taught us that even a revolt
which is based on simple compassion
can restore meaning to life . . .
(the way out) will not be found in books
and commentaries, but in encounters
with other men."[9]

At the deepest level, an identity crisis exposes ruling myths, higher education's concepts about man. The black critique rejects the "higher" view of education on matters black. Blacks demand that faculty and administrations share control of who will teach and what will be taught. The nonnegotiable interpretation of demands

[9] I. Silone, "The Choice of Companions," *Emergency Exit* (New York: Harper and Row, 1968), pp. 116–117.

grows out of omissions in the university's past, its de facto exclusions, the compromises for power, the normative void, unreasonableness in rationality (white attitudes . . . the myth of higher ruling?)'.

This is a demand to re-content influence, to challenge mere academic experience, to educate the old legitimacies. Bared myths ring as demands: the university has not demonstrated, by ideas or acts, its commitment to people. There is little reason to expect acceptance of a new commitment to those people most oppressed. W. H. Ferry has recently called for the creation of an all black college in California based on a new set of myths:

There are no issues in higher education
as pregnant with good and evil possibilities
as those presented by its growing black student body . . .
This potential impact is recognizable
in the courses in black history and language
and in the institutes and departments of black culture
here and there being hastily installed.
Some of these innovations
have been authorized out of expedience,
some out of fear,
many out of sympathy with black demands.

(Rebuttal?)

Yet all are makeshifts
that do not come to the heart of the difficulty,
which is black insistence
that the tradition and practice of higher education
are incorrigibly white
and inevitably directed at white goals
and that such an educational apparatus,
however benign its intentions,
cannot possibly achieve an outlook or program
that will meet permanently ignited black ambitions.[10]

[10] W. H. Ferry, "Letters to the Regents," *The Center Magazine*, 1969, 2(2).

This is the crisis in higher education. It smolders at many points in student rebellion, grievances over how institutions are governed, the underlying compromises which continuing support seems to make mandatory, the limits for comprehension in rationality which makes it on occasion unreasonable. But the crisis is most profound where it touches the ruling myths that higher education holds, which define itself as higher. The deepest roots of crisis are hardest for the highest educated to see.

The many facets of the crisis reveal erosion of the human dimension of life and suggest that this is a product of expanding knowledge. Zbigniew Brzezinski, among others, has recently posed the challenge of technetronics:

America . . . is becoming a technetronic society . . .
shaped culturally, psychologically, socially, and economically
by the impact of technology and electronics. . . .

This movement beyond the industrial phase is
separating America from the rest of the world
. . . the university is the creative eye of
the massive communication complex,
the source of much strategic planning,
domestic and international . . .
In these conditions, power will gravitate
increasingly into the hands of those who control
the information and can correlate it most rapidly. . . .

Accordingly, it will be essential
to put much emphasis on human values, lest personal
existence become increasingly depersonalized.
There is a real danger that human conduct will
become less spontaneous and less mysterious:
more predetermined and subject to deliberate
'programming.'

Whatever the outcome, American society . . . will be
the first tested. . . . Can the individual and science
coexist?[11]

[11] Z. Brzezinski, "National Economic Review," *New York Times,* January 6, 1969.

The threat of loss of human control looms at the very moment technology releases new and unprecedented power. Before technetronics there was already fear of machines. Historically, technology fostered priorities of production and efficiency which dislocated men. The readjustment was paid for in human costs: technological unemployment, technological wastes, pollution of water, air, and sound, spoilation of the natural environment, and depletion of the earth's resources. Harvey Wheeler writes on how the technicians of technology now threaten man more directly:

A shock reverberated through the intellectual establishment
of the West in the mid-twentieth century,
it became apparent that
science was not necessarily incompatible with totalitarianism.[12]

Technology, according to Marcuse, is forging one dimensional man:

The dominating reality is the technological octopus
conditioning our social, academic, and political institutions. . . .
Technology serves to institute new, more effective, and
more pleasant forms of social control . . .
the result is one rigidly predefined conceptual and behavior world.
Against this reality, rational protest is hopeless.[13]

Before it was work in order to consume and now increasingly it is consume in order to be able to work.

The other pincer against man, electronics, attacks through the expanded use of computers. The forty-five thousand computers now operating are expected soon to become household items. Almost everything can be quantified and retained, and computers have the capacity to learn from themselves. With electronic advance has also come a loss of personal privacy and the obliteration of the healing force of time. Wheeler goes on:

[12] H. Wheeler, "Bringing Science Under Law," *The Center Magazine,* 1969, *2*(11), 59.

[13] H. Marcuse, *One Dimensional Man* (Boston: Beacon, 1964), p. xv.

developments in mathematical logic, cybernation, systems analysis, and the planning-programming-budgeting approach to administrative control have been giving us reason of late to believe that a new science-spawned managerial revolution may yet be in the offing. New technology, of course, need not be a matter of concern unless another factor is present: that is the new technology and its practitioners must be engaged in the public interest. When this does not happen there are grave potentials for harming, as well as benefiting, society. . . . In setting our own house in order, we must face the serious problem that concerns our universities and the relationship between developmental science, and the proper approach to higher education. Revelations about Project Camelot and defense-oriented university research programs have made it obvious that developmental science has already distorted our educational processes and corrupted the idea of the university.[14]

But mainly the threat is in the myths, the ethic of the machine: preoccupation with efficiency, economy, predictability, and controls. Functioning alone, ungoverned by human goals, machine myths threaten man. Noam Chomsky has called this menace instrumentalism, and those who push the buttons the new mandarins:

power in our time
has more intelligence in its service
and allows that intelligence more discretion
than ever in history
we have moved to a society maimed
through the systematic corruption of intelligence

professionals
define problems according to the techniques
they have mastered
search for problems
to which their knowledge and skills
might be relevant
. . . the new mandarins

[14] Wheeler, *loc. cit.*, p. 60.

the largely humanist
occasionally ideologically-minded
intellectual dissenter
who sees his role
in terms of . . . social critique
is rapidly being replaced. . . .

organization-oriented, application-minded intellectuals
a new meritocratic elite
are taking over American life
using latest techniques
of communication and . . . technology.[15]

The failure of the university to form a counterweight to the military-industrial complex is one symptom. Isolated, this perversion of universality would be bad enough, but as part of a trend toward the management of intelligence, with intellectual managers in control of key decision points in information systems of power, it poses an ominous danger. The intellective, amplified without limit, comes out as oppression. With Vietnam and inner cities as cases in point, the critics have linked higher education into the military-industrial-university complex. An anti-human instrumentalism, critics charge, supports the status quo, denies that force is good for change, and enforces its decisions by violence it legitimizes.

Three million tons of bombs
more casualties than
World War II in all theaters and Korea
Victory still remote
but the land is dying . . .
for liberation.

Black consciousness, or the attitudes shaped by the black experience, enters here as a special legacy. While technetronics has been swallowing dissent, as Marcuse emphasizes, the black population has developed the capacity to speak out; as men are increasingly programmed into isolation and anomie, the black population

[15] N. Chomsky, "The Menace of Liberal Scholarship," *The New York Review of Books,* January 2, 1969.

has begun to organize; as many in the youth generation have turned to destroy the fabric of society, the black students have demanded that education and society evolve into what it now could be if human development was paramount. In a sense blacks, an obsolete people with respect to technetronics, loom as a creative resource when technetronics threatens those it has most related to. Norman Mailer has written about this black legacy:

the black man, living a life on the fringe
of technological society,
exploited by it, poisoned by it, half-rejected by it,
gulping prison air in the fluorescent nightmare of shabby
garish electric ghettos,
uprooted centuries ago from his native Africa,
his instincts living ergo
like nerves in the limbo of an amputated limb,
had thereby an experience unique to modern man—
he was forced to live at one and the same time
in the old primitive jungle of the slums,
and the hygienic surrealistic landscape of
technological society.
And he began to rise
from his exploitation,
He discovered
that the culture which had saved him owed more
to the wit and telepathy of the jungle
than the value and programs of the West.

His dance had taught him more
than writ and torts,
his music was sweeter
than Shakespeare or Bach
. . . the American Black . . . survived—
of all the peoples of the Western World,
he was the only one . . . of the twentieth century
to have undergone the cruel weeding of real survival.
So it was possible
his manhood had improved

while the manhood of others was being leached.
He had at any rate a vision.[16]

But threats against man are not the whole of technetronics. There is also the promise. Walter Ong reminds us of the new potential to be free from meaningless work and from many natural fears, to have power to act for good, to hope to end ignorance and even postpone death. Technetronics can have human meaning.

the age of technology
is part of the great and mysterious
evolution of the universe
devised by God . . . an epoch in . . . the
"hominization" of the world . . . taking over
of our planet by mankind . . .
this is clearly a highly bruited moment in history,
for the only alternative to using our freedom for fresh maturation
is allowing it to dissolve into mere anarchy.[17]

Bloy says even more pointedly:

man has come of age
no longer can claim dependency
he has the power and can respond
to himself and other men
He no longer can say, "I didn't know"
"It's not my responsibility."
God through technology,
has kicked man in the pants, and said,
"Grow Up!"[18]

This paper began by recognizing three apparent contradictions. This is the second, the appearance of conflict between technetronics and humanity. The threat to man, Ong and Bloy believe, can be turned to promise if the new power is turned to work for men. Technetronics could free men to face themselves. The ob-

[16] N. Mailer, *Look,* 1969, *33*(1), 60.
[17] M. B. Bloy, Jr., *Christian Century,* 1966, *85*(8), 232–233, quoting Walter Ong.
[18] In conversation with Bloy.

stacle is the absence of a commanding vision. The university should be the place, but technicians have little human vision and unavoidably promote not only postindustrial society, but also postethical culture. The possibility of liberation exists for man, but the question remains: how can the perspective of man come in and exert influence? In search of this how, we turn to the third apparent contradiction: the discovery of black uniqueness through reaching for universals. In this the black-conscious university takes on significance.

If it is true that blacks have improved, passed through the cruel weeding of a history written without them, if they have survived and stretched forth an insatiable zest for living, then perhaps their consciousness—black priorities and attitudes—can enrich higher education and offer a more human direction for machines.

There is some justification, as Ferry has pointed out, for a black-conscious university to come into being to promote pluralism in higher education:

It would be strange if our institutions
of higher education were not white-oriented.
A good deal of the problem rests in what we whites
think blacks should want.
We must pay strict attention to what the blacks say they want.
clinging to present standards is a counsel of futility
break down the Ph.D. fetishism.
much is to be said for students to have a voice
in the selection of their teachers . . .
no one knows whether there is a valid
black undergraduate experience
what we know is that current programs
were never designed with blacks in mind
the drive for black-conscious education is an intrinsic
and fundamental part of the quest for
self-respect, self-confidence, and independence.[19]

[19] Ferry, *loc. cit.* For additional information on Black Studies, see De Vere E. Pentony, "The Case for Black Studies," *Atlantic Monthly,* 1969, *223*(4), 81–89.

But what is this black consciousness, and consciousness of blackness? On the surface and from the outside it comes out of what is rejected (the WASPS, suburban living, powerlessness, oppression, establishments) and what is desired (Freedom Now, blacks leading, community organization). On a somewhat deeper level, black consciousness is a life style that includes full acceptance of oneself, of the obvious things in natural hair, soul food, and "doing our thing," but more deeply of the interior dimensions of conciousness and blackness which reveal a human outreach to the world.

The word black, in black consciousness, is a soulful word—it has deep tones and shadings. Black has many meanings but a single thrust, to be all-embracing. The universal quality of black is first in the nature of the color:

Black,
completest possible negation of white,
to allow absorption of every color
and yet it reflects the least amount of color
black, paradoxically, the absence of color.

When the reference is to people, blacks are men oppressed, and yet who is free? Blacks are:

Negroes, former Africans, a few of them are black.
Colonialized peoples, the colored majority in the world beyond the West.
Peoples anywhere oppressed, many of whom are unknown and unsung though white.

Tomorrow's man struggling against the technetronic master.

history is the history of
man's attempt to fulfill his blackness,
his resistance to being reduced
to producer, consumer . . .
producing finally the atomic bomb
which awaits to consume him.[20]

[20] S. Wynter, "Reflections on West India Writing and Criticism," *Jamaica Journal,* 1968, *2*(12), 30.

Blacks are people of any color who are consciously dedicated to emancipation, civil rights, shared interdependence, freedom for human fulfillment. The black priority is pro-people. Listen to Fanon:

> *Every time a man has contributed to the victory of the dignity of the spirit, every time a man has said no to attempts to subjugate his fellows, I have felt solidarity with his act.*[21]

Lerone Bennett, Jr., underscores the black-conscious task of conscience, and the black man's unique role as America's conscience.

> *I know that blacks need more money*
> *. . . still there must be a* via media *. . . the black man's task*
> *to show America . . . America's Faustian obsession*
> *with money and power . . . to recognize that*
> *the essence of Faustianism is a deal involving*
> *not money or power but the soul.*
>
> *to avoid the pitfall, one must transcend*
> *not only the oppressor but the values of oppression*
> *the black man who accepts completely*
> *the success and power ethic*
> *must also hate himself*
> *for there is no defense for an unavenged defeat*
>
> *Not free from what, but free for what?*
> *A large number of blacks—many of them Freedom Fighters—*
> *are attacking not only segregation but hypocrisy*
> *black and white*
> *asking not only for human dignity but for a society*
> *open to all of the creative possibilities in man.*
>
> *by the grace of God and the whip of history*
> *black people, in the main, have not completely*
> *assimilated those values that are driving Western man*
> *to social and spiritual suicide:*

[21] F. Fanon, *Black Skins, White Masks* (New York: Grove, 1967), p. 226.

the acquisitiveness . . .
numbness of heart and machine idolatry.
to the extent that these things are foreign
to the black experience
to that extent the black man is uniquely qualified
to take the lead in recasting the human values
of our civilization.[22]

To become conscious of people as blacks requires looking to the human things, to the humanities, and especially the arts which illuminate man's inside dimension. Carolyn F. Gerald speaks of black literature:

the image we have of ourselves
controls what we are capable of doing.
Image, in this sense, has the meaning
of self-concept . . . the mirror
of some aspect of reality

for the most part . . . black writers (. . . or writers
who write black)
. . . contributing to our growing sense of peoplehood
what is new (in blackened literature?)
is the deliberate desecration and
smashing of idols, the turning inside-out
of symbols . . .
Bitterness . . . being replaced by wrath;
a sense of power which proceeds
from a mythic consciousness based
on a people's positive view of themselves
and their destiny.[23]

A black poet in residence at Cornell adds:

Blackwriting . . . the result of centuries
of slavery and forced alienation

[22] L. Bennett, Jr., "A Certain Dark Joy," *Ebony,* 1968, *24*(12), 42–44.

[23] C. F. Gerald, "The Black Writer and His Role," *Negro Digest,* 1969, *18*(4), 42–47.

from Africa and one's-self . . .
exiles in a strange land where our whole
life style . . . comes into contradiction . . .

Blackart is a functional art . . .
committed to humanism . . .
out of a concrete situation
everyday things which make
up the texture of life . . .
people . . . help to shape the art
. . . until its full meaning has been achieved.[24]

The premachine origins reemerge. Art in tribal life is a functional element of the social machinery, not an escape, but part of an authentic whole. Its uses give it its aesthetic. Art is produced by people for people, not for an elite, or for market, or for a machine. In black art, LeRoi Jones writes, people are beating their way back to the natural, trying to relink art and essential reality. Jones adds:

those brothers in Cleveland . . .
they were beating drums . . .
they called the thing down
the Divinity spoke to them,
after awhile they came
face to face
with what it was symbolizing.
sometimes it seems terrible or beautiful,
or spooky,
because it brings something into being
something you might lose consciousness of
by being involved with just earthy things[25]

Max Roach explains similar stirrings produced by jazz:

"Jazz" is an extension of . . . African chants . . .
of the pain and suffering

[24] D. L. Lee, "Black Writing: this is u, thisisu," *Negro Digest,* 1969, *18*(5), 51–52, 78–81.

[25] L. Jones, "Islam and Black Art," *Negro Digest,* 1969, *18*(3), 8.

emotional intensity, brilliance, and drive
[which tell] where the "Negro" came from . . .
and foretell where he might go one day.
[Jazz] . . . comes out of the experience,
suffering, and love of the black people . . .
No intellectual analysis . . . will work for a reproduction
of the emotional tools of feeling he used.[26]

Consciousness provides an experience of something deep and alive that says, "This is the real me!" Consciousness of self comes at moments of special awareness, the inner synthesis, revelatory experiences. At the same time, this inner consciousness makes real the whole of humanity and the process of humanization of the world. Ruth Nanda Anshen writes:

It is this thesis . . . that man . . .
is developing a new consciousness
which . . . can eventually lift the human race . . .
above . . . the fear,
ignorance and isolation which beset it today . . .
this nascent consciousness . . .
that beyond the divisiveness among men
there exists a primordial unitive power
since we are all bound together
by a common humanity
more fundamental than any unity or dogma,
the forces which have scattered
and atomized mankind . . . replaced
by an integrating structure
capable of bestowing meaning and purpose on existence . . .
that ecumenical power of the mind and heart . . .
realization that spirit and nature
are not separate and apart . . .
intuition and reason . . . fusing
inner being with outer reality
the conception of wholeness, unity, organism
an enlarged meaning of life

[26] M. Roach, "Jazz," *Freedom Ways,* 1962, *2*(2), 173–176.

Knowledge no longer consists
in manipulations of man and
nature as opposite forces,
nor in the reduction of data to
mere statistical order
but as a means of liberating
mankind
from the destructive power
of fear
toward the rehabilitation of the
human will

the ultimate answer to the hopes
and fears which pervade
modern society
rest on the moral fiber of man
perception
that the individual person and
the collective person
supplement and integrate
each other.[27]

union can only increase
through increase in conscious-
ness
that is to say in vision . . .
vision is fuller being
power acquired by a conscious-
ness
to turn in upon itself,
to take
possession of itself as an object
no longer merely to know,
but to know oneself . . . a
new sphere
as it explodes onto itself[28]

The incipient development of
mankind into a single pool of
thought . . .
inter-thinking humanity . . .
a new type of organism . . .
to realize new possibilities
for evolving life
on this planet[29]

The essence of consciousness is soul, the essentially human.

soul is what, forever, has made black people hip.
and it is what has enticed whites to imitate them
without understanding it.
Among black people soul is congenital understanding
and respect for each other.
It is the knowledge that one is
but a segment of all that is
. . . like the colors in a rainbow;
it is a deep purple haze . . . like morning . . . like dusk.
yet like when its colors are all rolled into one

[27] In Silone, *op. cit.,* pp. ix–xiii.
[28] de Chardin, *op. cit.,* pp. 28 and 165.
[29] *Ibid.,* p. 20 in Introduction by Sir Julian Huxley.

It makes you humble, peaceful.
That is why, above all,
soul is wise and weary . . .
it is the sophistication that knows
better than to ask, "Understand me," and settles instead for
"Don't mess with me; I'm in my own thing, Baby."[30]

I hesitate to try to define soul or vision or hominization more than to say that they embody this consciousness, the turning inward that permits a reaching outward. Having black consciousness involves this fierce embracing of oneself as a living whole. Black consciousness makes sense for Negroes but does it not also ring true for . . . and especially those threatened by . . . Listen to yourself . . . is this message separatist? (or are white attitudes?) Do not the black word and the human word humanize? Listen to yourself being in black-conscious terms.

The black (human) man . . .
rejects finally from himself
his own resentment of being black.
(human)
This is a profound . . . universal
theme, . . .
achievement of personal integrity
and wholeness . . . connected . . .
with being black.
Because the Negro is despised . . .
for his black skin . . .
the only escape is . . . to affirm
his own blackness . . .

Because our color (black
and white)
has been used as a weapon
to oppress us
we must use our color
as a weapon of liberation[31]

[30] C. Brown and A. Calloway, "Soul," *Esquire,* 1968, *59*(4), 88. In a related vein, de Chardin writes: "Without the slightest doubt *there is something* through which material and spiritual energy hold together and are complementary. In the last analysis, *somehow or other,* there must be a single energy operating in the world. And the first idea that occurs to us is that the 'soul' must be as it were a focal point of transformation at which, from all points of nature, the forces of bodies converge, to become interiorised and sublimated in beauty and truth." *Op. cit.,* p. 63.

[31] S. Carmichael, quoted by J. H. Clarke, "Black Power and Black History," *Negro Digest,* 1969, *18*(4), 14.

Negritude emerges from
intense personal experience . . .
not a matter of self-justification
but of defiant self-acceptance[32]

the new (black) consciousness
newly-gained self confidence
the blackened outlook on life
'an antiracist racism'
the moment of negativity as reaction
to . . . white supremacy . . . an ultimate synthesis
of a common humanity without racism.[33]

"I am not really a Pan-Africanist. I am a Humanist."[34] "The ideal of the black personality: to feel myself . . . myself."

Black
as the gentle night
Black
as the kind and quiet night
Black
as the deep and productive
earth.
Body
Out of Africa,
Strong and black . . .
Kind
As the black night
My song
From the dark lips
Of Africa
Beautiful
As the black night . . .

God
glad I'm black
pitch-forking devil black:
black, black, black;
black absolute of life complete,
greedfully grabbing life's
living,
stupor drunkenness,
happiness.
depth of hurt,
anger of sorrow:
synthesis of joy, sadness;
composite child of life.[35]

[32] C. Legum, *Pan Africanism: A Short Political Guide* (New York: Praeger, 1962), p. 93.

[33] Legum, *op. cit.*, p. 95.

[34] *Ibid.*, quoting Leopold Senghor, p. 95.

[35] B. Modisane, "Black Beauty," *Look,* 1969, *33*(1), from poem "blue black," 74.

Black
Out of Africa
Me and my song.[36]

As I face Africa I ask myself:
what is it between us
that constitutes a tie
which I can feel
better than I can explain?
. . . The real essence of this kinship
is the social heritage of slavery;
the discrimination and insult;
. . . binds together not simply
the children of Africa,
but extends through
yellow Asia and into the South Seas.[37]
(and to you)

Black deals with oppression by turning it to identity.
Black is one color which embraces all colors elevating none

Blacks are Negroes, Africans, Asians . . . under white oppression
and whites oppressed by Negroes, Africans, Asians . . .
or other whites
Blacks are people powered enough to overcome their lack of power
and peopled enough to overcome the price of power.

The black man is the man who accepts himself as man.

All this is heady and earthy, or, as indicated at the outset, soulful. If poetic exceptions are allowed, the thrust of the black thing is toward a universality which embraces all who affirm the species in its deepest psychic dimensions. The black message which provides a healing for Negroes can unite all those men who can

[36] *Ibid.*, quoting L. Hughes, p. 18.
[37] W. E. B. Du Bois, *Dusk of Dawn* (New York: Schocken, 1940), pp. 116–117.

accept a black dimension in themselves. Fanon, DuBois, and Malcolm all understood this universality in black consciousness once they came to their full understanding. To be black is to be political but it is also to have an inner peace, the ability to live with oneself. Perhaps only with self in hand can men move on to live as part of others.

A black-conscious university would attempt to bring together in better balance knowledge and spirit. It would provide a humanization of intellectuality and temper the interests of the elite with the insights of the masses. In its curriculum it would be heavily comparative, relating the poor to the rich, the West to the world.

it would have a comparative perspective . . .
historical and cultural experiences of the poor with the affluent . . .
the American . . . in the world experience
the Judaeo-Christian to the Islamic and eastern world views.
Emphasis upon those parts of the world which have received
little attention
Latin America, Africa, Asia . . .
. . . the experiences of the outside, of the exploited and
the marginal . . .

heavily engaged in service
resources available to others whose needs were not just
obvious and neglected, but whose very experience
of being constrained
would give promise of heightened human sensitivity

havens for the critics,
support for assaults on those who
dehumanize man
through technological, religious, racial,
or economic means
oriented toward promoting productive human relations
in place of improving products or assuring profits

breakdown of barriers
between campus and community

nation and nation
man and mankind.[38]

Negro Digest recently gave details of the dimensions of the black university:

The concept is revolutionary . . . breaking out . . .
where existing universities are scholar-oriented,
the Black University will be community-oriented
where the traditional university has emphasized the intellectual
and cultural development of the student toward academic excellence
and elitism, the Black University will seek to involve the total
community in its reach toward unity, self-determination,
the acquisition and use of political and economic power . . .
the protection of the human spirit[39]

Edgar F. Beckham adds:

the Black University . . . the product of visionaries,
who affirm the validity of Black experience . . .
In short, the Black University exists implicitly wherever and
whenever Black people join together for a Black educational
purpose. As process and as people, the Black University
has only two critical characteristics: freedom from extraneous
influence and committed responsiveness to the educational needs
of Black people . . . for the liberation of Black men's minds
and souls.[40]

Along with the word *veritas* the black conscious university would place the word *muntu,* a Bantu word of inclusive character having to do with man as a spiritual being, transcendent, invested with that most precious quality, humanity, which is law unto itself, natural

[38] Elaboration of comments made in *Black Consciousness and Higher Education,* an occasional publication of the Church Society for College Work, Cambridge, Mass., 1968, p. 19.

[39] H. W. Fuller, "Toward a Black University," *Negro Digest,* 1969, *18*(5), 4.

[40] E. F. Beckham, "Problems of 'Place' Personnel and Practicality," *Negro Digest, 18*(5), 25 and 29.

and insuperable, and forever possessed of precedence over things, order, and property.[41]

So toned and shaded—blackened with a human consciousness—the university might well emerge from its crisis as a force capable of responding to the technetronic strain—a black vision might shine through, the darkness might be light enough.

[41] J. Jahn, *Muntu* (New York: Grove, 1961).

Index